Teachers and Special Educational Needs:

Coping with change

Edited by
Mike Hinson

SECOND EDITION

Longman
in association with National Association for
Remedial Education

Longman Industry and Public Service Management, Longman
Group UK Ltd, The High, Harlow, Essex CM20 1YR, England and
Associated Companies throughout the world
Telephone Harlow (0279) 442601; Fax Harlow (0279) 444501; Telex
81491 Padlog

First published 1989, Second edition 1991

A catalogue record for this book is available from the British
Library

ISBN 0-582-08673-6 Second edition
ISBN 0-582-00405-5 First edition

Printed and bound in Great Britain by
Biddles Ltd, Guildford and King's Lynn

19-99

C/R
STL
519
TEA

Contents

iv

List of Contributors

Mike Hinson Freelance editor, writer and education consultant. From January 1979 to August 1991 he was Head of SENASS, Child Psychology Service, Sandwell MBC. Mike Hinson is a Past President of NARE, is the Association's Publications Editor, and was founding Editor of the journal *Support for Learning*. His other publications include: *Encouraging Results* (1978 Macdonald Educational); *Planning Effective Progress* (with Martin Hughes, 1982 Hulton) and *Teachers and Special Educational Needs* (1987 Longman).

John Acklaw Chief Inspector, Essex County Council.

Terence Bailey Senior Adviser for Special Education, London Borough of Enfield.

Tricia Barthorpe Head of Scunthorpe Learning Support Services, Humberside. She is a member of the Mathematics Association's Diploma Board and was President of NARE, 1990—1991.

Graham Bill Head of Learning Support Service (Western Area), Gloucestershire County Council.

Mary Bland Head of Learning Coordination Team, T.P. Riley Community School, Walsall Metropolitan Borough Council, West Midlands.

Stewart Bourne Head of Sandwell Assessment of Achievement Unit, Sandwell Metropolitan Borough Council, West Midlands.

Elizabeth Cowne Head of Learning Support Service, London Borough of Merton.

Christopher Dyer General Inspector for Special Educational Needs, London Borough of Newham. Honorary Secretary, National Association of Advisory Officers for Special Education.

Charles Gains Editor of *Support for Learning* and a Past President of NARE.

Yash Gupta Senior Educational Psychologist, Essex County Council.

Gill Hackett Advisory Teacher for Primary English, Sandwell Metropolitan Council, with responsibility for the LINC (Language in the National Curriculum) Project.

Graham Harris Head of Science, Darlaston Community School, Walsall Metropolitan Borough Council.

Ann Klotz Peripatetic Support Teacher with Kingston Reading Centre, London Borough of Kingston-on-Thames.

Gerry Lewis Head of Service for Children with Learning Difficulties, Northamptonshire County Council.

Colin J. Smith Senior Lecturer, School of Education, University of Birmingham.

Gary Thomas Senior Lecturer, School of Education, Oxford Polytechnic. He is Reviews Editor of *Support for Learning*.

John Visser Principal Lecturer and Staff Development Tutor, Westhill College, Birmingham. He is a Past President of NARE.

Phil Watts Principal Educational Psychologist, Sandwell Metropolitan Borough Council.

Joseph Winterbourne Coordinator for Special Needs Support, George Salter High School, West Bromwich, Sandwell Metropolitan Borough Council.

Acknowledgements

The editors and publishers gratefully acknowledge permission given by Basil Blackwell to publish articles by John Acklaw and Yash Gupta, and Terence Bailey which originally appeared in *Support for Learning*, Vol 6, No 1, February 1991.

They also wish to express their gratitude to Phil Watts for permission to reproduce figure 12.3, the daily planner, and figure 12.4, the task tracker; to George Salter High School, West Bromwich for permission to reproduce figures 3.1, 3.2, 3.3, 3.4 and 3.5, also to Julia Sanders for her help and advice concerning word processing.

Introduction

Mike Hinson

During a twenty-year partnership with NARE, Longman has published not only the Association's journal, but also three successful books: *Remedial Education: Programmes and Progress* (1977), *Remedial Education: Guidelines for the Future* (1979), and *Teachers and Special Educational Needs* (1987). Each was concerned with the improvement of provision for children in mainstream education who have special educational needs.

By the summer of 1990, stock of the third title had been completely sold out. After a careful review of the contents, it was decided that, in the light of rapid developments in education, neither a reprinting nor a revised edition was feasible. At that stage, the publisher invited me to compile a completely new book relevant to the present special educational scene. I was glad to accept that invitation and it gives me great pleasure to introduce *Teachers and Special Educational Needs: Coping with Change*.

Educational reform

Without doubt, the most momentous piece of educational legislation to be enacted in recent years is the Education Reform Act 1988. Its credo is that higher standards in education will be achieved by making each school responsible and publicly accountable for what it does.

Implicit in ERA, is the right of every pupil of compulsory school age attending a maintained or grant maintained school to a broad and balanced curriculum based on the National Curriculum. The principle that those with special educational needs should share this common entitlement with their peers has taken many years to gain acceptance, a process with which readers of this book will be all too familiar. Achieving maximum access to the National Curriculum for these pupils and securing their subsequent progress will, in the words of *A Curriculum for All* (1989) 'challenge the cooperation, understanding and planning skills of teachers, support agencies, parents and governors and many others'.

The power to make temporary exceptions to the curriculum is extended to all headteachers. Under Section 19 of ERA, a directive may be issued which excepts an individual child from part or all of the National Curriculum for six months, in the first instance. Both the Secretary of State for Education and the National Curriculum Council have expressed the view that 'exceptional arrangements' ought to be kept to a minimum. The process involved is correspondingly tortuous.

Mindful that considerable LEA staffing and financial resources are devoted to special educational needs, the DES in a draft circular issued in 1990, registered its intention to review staffing arrangements in order to maintain them at optimum efficiency. The Secretary of State considered that every school should be able to call upon the expertise of a member of staff who had specific responsibility for SEN pupils. The circular underlined the policy of encouraging the provision of in-service training in order to give such teachers 'a level of qualification appropriate to their responsibilities'.

HM Inspectorate issued its report, *A Survey of Pupils with Special Educational Needs in Ordinary Schools* in December 1989. It found that, in schools where a whole-school policy for special educational needs had been developed, and which was actively supported by senior management and appropriately qualified staff, there had been a positive influence on the quality of work from pupils. Even though, at that time, one third of primary and secondary schools still needed to review their arrangements, the survey clearly revealed that the issue of teaching pupils with SEN was a priority in many schools, with a consequent improvement in both ethos and educational standards.

The most radical feature of the 1988 Education Act has been the implementation of local management of schools (LMS). Each local education authority has been required to devise a formula for the delegation of responsibility for the school budget to all secondary schools and all primary schools with more than 200 pupils on roll. There are discretionary powers to give similar responsibilities to smaller schools and special schools. School governors, in consultation with the headteacher, are now responsible for the management of the school budget and for management decisions affecting the school's staffing. The thrust of these changes has been to inject a competitive dimension into school management and organisation. Even though the workload of the National Curriculum is heavy, it is perhaps the ramifications of LMS that have done more to cause concern and stress in the teaching profession.

The changing role of teachers

In 1985, NARE published its booklet, *Teaching Roles for Special Educational Needs*. This reaffirmed the Association's conviction that the needs of children with learning difficulties must be the responsibility of the whole staff in every school, also advocating that each should be led by a specially appointed and trained coordinator. The statement identified seven broad areas in the role of a special needs teacher: assessment, prescription, teaching and pastoral, supporting colleagues, liaison, management and staff development. *Teachers and Special Educational Needs* (1987) provided a more detailed discussion of these areas, grouping them under five interdependent section headings, also substituting the term *intervention* for that of *prescription*.

As can be seen from the summary of the HMI Report mentioned previously, much has been achieved since then. The notion of a whole school approach has become both meaningful and operative in the majority of schools. Others have continued to refine their policies since the publication of the Report.

This explains why a revision of the 1987 handbook would not have been appropriate. Whilst the broad areas of the teacher's role remain equally relevant, current changes and concerns have led to a different degree of emphasis being necessary in each of them. The main chapters in this new book have been contributed by writers with a wide range of practical experience, all of whom have a proven commitment to special educational needs. Where appropriate, these chapters have been supplemented with accounts of good practice recently published in *Support for Learning*.

Supporting teachers: coping with change

In this introductory section, I deal with the fundamental role of teachers and schools as agents of change, placing it in the context of special educational needs. Basic procedures for managing changes are discussed, including the use of Force Field analysis as a problem-solving technique. Consideration is also given to ways of coping with stress at both personal and organisational levels.

Assessment and intervention

During the summer of 1991, pupils at National Curriculum Key Stage 1 experienced SATs in the core curriculum areas. Modifications had been made to the procedures originally trialled in 1990. (Further modifications are in hand for 1992.) Most teachers, it seems, have felt very like Alice who, you will recall in *Through the Looking Glass*, had to run very hard to stay in the same square. Stewart Bourne makes a critical overview of the first two years of National Curriculum. He examines the implications of its implementation, delivery, assessment, record-keeping and reporting with particular reference to pupils with special educational needs. He concludes by advancing provisional criteria for assessing its effectiveness.

In the secondary school in which he has served for more than ten years, Joseph Winterbourne has played a key role in changing a highly effective remedial department into a school service which provides a range of support across the curriculum. His procedures for collecting and disseminating information will be of interest to readers in both primary and secondary schools.

Teachers and support in action

This section begins with Christopher Dyer's discussion of the purposes and nature of support. He shares his conviction that by categorising the forms of support that are possible, they can then be more precisely targeted at particular learning difficulties.

Charles Gains identifies those elements of possible meta-model which are necessary for meeting the curricular needs of pupils with learning difficulties. Tricia Barthorpe follows with her discussion of the broad, balanced, relevant and differentiated curriculum.

Although they are noted in schools with increasing frequency, examples of good practice emerge in print rather more slowly. Teachers often need a great deal of encouragement to set down accounts of their achievements in adapting curricula, or in supporting special needs pupils to cope in the mainstream situation. The three articles reprinted in this section are particularly relevant. Mary Bland and Graham Harris describe the introduction of peer tutoring to science lessons. Gill Hackett reports on a project in which collaborative writing developed with a group of Year 5 and Year 6 children who have found writing a difficult process. A cross-phase, cross-curricular initiative known as *The Settlers Project* is described by Ann Klotz and Elizabeth Cowne. Much of its content would be appropriate to Programmes of Study in history and geography.

Two topical contributions on the work of support services round off this section. Gerry Lewis gives practical examples of their work and then goes on to discuss the future role of learning support services. Clearly, their future lies very much in the hands of the schools which they support. As head of a large multi-disciplinary team, Phil Watts considers a possible set of entitlements for all parties involved in support services' work.

Management

Management issues are very much to the fore in education at present and the three chapters included in this section are devoted to major issues of current concern. I follow my introductory chapter on aspects of change with a survival guide to time management and the management of meetings. The current climate of change has brought an increased workload for all who work in education. The way to cope effectively with this is to make best use of the time available, of which meetings seem to occupy a disproportionate share.

The Elton Report, *Discipline in Schools*, published by the DES in 1989, has perhaps not received the prominence which it deserves. Yet 'behaviour management in the classroom' seems to be one of the most popular subjects for professional training days. Based on evidence gathered from a wide range of sources, the Elton Report concluded that most schools are well run, that school-based influences on behaviour are very important, and that the most effective schools appear to have created a positive atmosphere based on a sense of community and shared values. Colin Smith discusses the implications of developing a whole-school policy for coping with behaviour problems.

In his chapter, Gary Thomas argues that special needs educators have spent too much time developing special methods of assessment and teaching. His research has shown that some special needs can be met simply by making significant changes to the organisation of a classroom.

Liaison

The chairperson of one governing body is reported as having stated that, fundamentally, governors represent the community of a particular school. Those who earn their living within the school need to be able to rely on governors 'to hold up a mirror of the world outside school to the world inside school'. The enhanced powers of the governing body and its crucial role in school management extend to children with special educational needs and members of staff with particular responsibility for their welfare. This being so, every effort should be made to create a fruitful partnership with governors. In his chapter, Graham Bill explores the situation and gives some practical guidelines for achieving this end.

Recent legislation has done much to enhance parents' rights, thereby recognising the stake which they have in the education of their children. In their article, John Acklaw and Yash Gupta argue that even though educationalists' views on dyslexia differ, they are all likely to recognise that a very real problem exists. Taking this as an example, they tackle the question of how misunderstandings between school and parents can be averted, and appropriate help and support offered.

Staff development

Arguably, one of the most positive encouragements to the enhancement of teachers' professional knowledge and expertise has been the introduction of professional training days. Personal experience shows that they have been utilised very effectively for giving staffs a greater awareness of special educational needs and in implementing whole-school policies. However, their scope is limited. John Visser writes a frank appraisal of the current situations in both pre-service training courses and advanced courses. He looks into the future and suggests measures which need to be taken if an adequate number of additionally qualified special needs teachers is to be maintained.

There is a developing interest in classroom observation techniques. Traditional barriers are breaking down as teachers come to recognise the need to improve their delivery systems. Terence Bailey has produced his own 'nudge sheet'. He suggests a number of practical ways in which classroom procedures can be reviewed in a professional manner.

Accepting the challenge

In the four short years that have elapsed since the publication of *Teachers and Special Educational Needs*, we have all been participants in the biggest upheaval in education since the implementation of the 1944 Education Act. It is clear that both children with special needs and their teachers have gained a greater acceptance as members of the school community. Although reactionary enclaves still exist in schools, generally speaking they are now regarded as part of the school's ethos, as opposed to being seen as an embarrassment. This means that both teachers and pupils are as much part of the maelstrom of change as everyone else.

This book attempts to address some of the changes. It presents a blend of discussion, critical appraisal and practical advice. Our target readership is teachers in mainstream schools who are concerned with special educational needs. The book is also for teacher trainers, advisers and administrators. There are no 'cook book' answers to problems. *Teachers and Special Educational Needs: Coping with Change* has been written by a group of concerned professionals, working in close cooperation, who have attempted to maintain NARE's traditional balance in its publications of theory combined with sound practice. We sincerely hope that readers will find it stimulating, even provocative, and of considerable practical use.

Part I
Supporting teachers:
coping with change

1 Aspects of coping with change

Mike Hinson

Times past

I hadn't known my son-in-law's father for very long before I discovered that we had both attended the same grammar school. He had left in 1937, I had begun in 1945. Recollections revealed that, despite the disruption of World War II, we had shared the same teachers for the same lessons and that the school had changed very little in those intervening years. It seemed that neither lessons nor timetables had changed much. Staff changes were few — the masters who returned from the war had taught at the school before being called-up. Several of the older masters had attended the school as boys. After a spell at university (and as soldiers in the Great War) they had returned to the school as members of staff, and remained there until their retirement.

Time moved on and, in 1956 as a young teacher in my first job, I joined the staff of a secondary modern school which thought itself 'progressive'. (Providing one remembered which chair to sit on in the staffroom, everything was fine.) The headteacher had been in the post for ten years. In deference to the 1944 Education Act, he had evolved a system which took some account of education according the boys' age ability and aptitude — and from which he was loath to depart.

In summarising the origins of change, Reddin (1970) sets out the main characteristics of what he terms a *frozen organisation*:

— senior staff have remained in one job for years;
— promotion is by seniority;

— the rule book is enormous;
— past practice is regarded as the safest guideline to follow;
— innovation and creativity are viewed with suspicion and tend to be suppressed.

Based on these criteria, the two schools appear, with hindsight, to be archetypal examples of frozen educational organisations, having remained at permafrost intensity for many years, despite a brief thaw around 1946. To be fair, the schools were typical of many others of their day, functioning reasonably effectively within the educational tenets of the time. Changes such as the change from School Certificate examinations to GCE or the introduction of CSE examinations in the 1960s did not make undue demands on the basic systems in operation.

Thirty-five years on

On reflection, any teething troubles experienced by those schools pale into insignificance compared with the present, ever-accelerating sequence of changes that all schools have been experiencing since the implementation of the Education Act, 1988.

Griffiths (1975) puts forward the proposition that the major impetus for change in organisations comes from outside, however, Reddin (op cit) regards *legislated change* as one of the less effective ways of bringing it about. Legislated change usually takes the form of an edict from the top or from outside the organisation. It can be made more difficult if the organisation is currently operating in a reasonably efficient manner or if the reason for change is difficult to explain. Many of the changes that schools now face stem from legislation. The schools' task is to convert political decisions embodied in legislation, in addition to their commitment to higher standards, into effective professional practice.

All would accept that the fundamental purpose of schools is to develop their pupils' potential through a structured process of learning and personal development. This being so, the organisational structure of each school should be such that it becomes an agency for change whilst its staff, working both as individuals and as a team, become change agents. In the past, this aspect of educational management has received less attention than it deserves, the reason for this being that the aims of the school have been fulfilled mainly by what teachers have achieved in their classrooms. As a result, management of change in schools has been too dependent upon the enthusiasm of individuals who have needed to expend much effort in promoting staff goodwill and cooperation in order that a particular initiative should become accepted. The changes now taking place are so demanding and extensive that it has become necessary to adopt a more efficient management process. There is a necessity to utilise the collective potential of the whole staff in the initiation of change and development. This approach calls for efficient management from the top downwards.

In addition to professional competence, the management of change will require greater attention to interpersonal skills and organisational strategies than has been the case in the past. As an example, the reaching of a consensus requires practice in the skills of persuasion, negotiation and team-building.

Special educational needs and change

For many years many primary and secondary schools remained frozen organisations as far as children with special educational needs were concerned. Limited expectations of their ability to benefit from the normal school system were perpetuated. The responsibility for coping with their needs was frequently abdicated to 'someone else' — a special group or class, a peripatetic teacher, or a special school. Remedial teachers had often worked in enforced isolation, other teachers' expectations of their professional competence often being on a par with their prejudices about the children. Whilst the overall results of Brennan's enquiry for Schools Council (1979) were damning, they nevertheless identified pockets of excellence, nurtured by dedicated teachers who had the ability to enthuse colleagues with their commitment to children with learning difficulties.

The recommendations of the Warnock Report (1978), enacted by the Education Act 1981, brought about legislative changes which in the case of special education have had beneficial consequences. The Act stated that the aims of education were the same for *all* pupils, the 1988 Education Act later confirming their equal right to a broad and balanced curriculum, including the National Curriculum. ERA also placed considerable power in the hands of governors, at the same time clearly outlining their responsibilities to the children with special needs in the schools that they served.

Its hand strengthened by major legislation, the cause of special education steadily advanced during the 1980s. In mainstream schools, the adoption of a whole school approach to children's special educational needs was encouraged and, in many instances, successfully implemented.

However, the enthusiastic proclamation of that simple phrase 'whole school approach' has become a panacea, the deep underlying implications for the philosophy, methodology and organisation of any school which decides to adopt it often having been overlooked.

A whole school policy for anything, not least special educational needs, sets a tough agenda when the precepts, principles and prejudices of other colleagues come to be challenged. There is likely to be some 'sales resistance' with which the designated change agents will have to grapple.

On becoming a change agent

Attempts to induce changes in any system are likely to encounter some form of blocking or resistance by those who want to preserve the status quo. Notwithstanding, it is important to recognise that resistance to change is a natural phenomenon and does not stem solely from sheer obstinacy. To a greater or lesser degree the prospect of change evokes fears in everyone, for example, the fear that one will not be able to cope or that one's sense of professional competence will be eroded. There is a natural tendency for individuals to want to protect their integrity and identity. A change programme will have a greater chance of success if these factors are taken into account.

Robson and Wright (1989) warn against potential change agents donning the mantle of the 'mythical hero-innovator', thereby regarding themselves as 'taking the gospel of special educational treatment to a hostile and uncomprehending world'. Therefore, before embarking upon any course of action which might lead to change, the intending change agents would be wise to examine carefully their own preparedness for such a task. Stewart (1983) lists a number of qualities shared by good managers of change including:

— they know clearly what they want to achieve;
— they can see proposed changes not only from their own viewpoint but also from that of others;
— they don't mind being out on a limb;
— they harness circumstances to enable change to be implemented;
— they involve colleagues in the management of change and protect their security;
— they make change personally rewarding for people, wherever possible;
— they share maximum information about possible outcomes.

Reviewing the situation

For sustained and effective change to develop, the needs of not only the organisation but also of the group and its individual members must be taken into account at every stage.

An early review of the current situation is an important precursor to initiating change. For example, if the proposed change is that of engendering a whole school approach to special educational needs, the review will generate a number of questions which will need to be answered, such as:

—What is our level of commitment to such a change?
—How much support amongst the staff is there?
—What skills and knowledge do we have at our disposal?
—How much time do we have available?
—How well will we cope as change agents?
—How will we work together?

and so forth.

Figure 1.1 Top twenty objections to change

1. Why change when things are going along so nicely?
2. We've got enough to do as it is.
3. If only we had the time ...
4. You can't teach old dogs new tricks.
5. That's not going to do anything to solve *our* problems.
6. Nothing new about that — we've been doing it for . . .* years.
7. We tried it once before and it didn't work.
8. We haven't the specialist staff for that at present.
9. This requires extensive and thorough analysis before we do anything.
10. It won't work in a small school.
11. It won't work in a large school.
12. No one has ever tried it before.
13. We haven't got the money for it at present.
14. It's only another bandwagon.
15. The staff won't accept it.
16. It's not in line with school policy.
17. It's not in the best interest of the pupils.
18. I believe in it in principle, but ...
19. I have never been one for standing in the way of progress but . . .
20. What's the point? I shall be retiring in . . .* years time.

*Insert an appropriate figure between 1 and 40 in the space provided.

A clear picture of the school's state of readiness is vital, also of how well such a change can be integrated into the current work load.

It is likely that such a review will reveal several areas which need attention prior to 'going public'. In the event of an 'all clear' to proceed, the review process will also have helped to clarify the overall aim or goal. In our example, therefore, if the goal is for the school to adopt a whole school policy, it must be made clear to all participants that, whatever their level of involvement with special needs has been previously, they are about to become involved in a shared, pro-active approach in future.

Moving forward

In order to achieve and sustain effective change, it will be necessary to persuade people to behave differently from the way in which they have acted in the past. Remember that unless behaviour changes, nothing changes. One of the most important motivating forces is that of getting all concerned involved in the change process and in discussing the reasons for it. At an early stage, it is important to build up a clear picture of the factors which will be helpful to progress, equally of those which might prove to be a hindrance. One systematic problem-solving strategy often used is an adaptation of Lewin's Force Field Analysis (1935, 1947). This is shown diagrammatically in figure 1.2, the method for undertaking such an analysis being as follows:

1. Having identified your goal, use 'brainstorming' to identify the *driving forces*, that is those forces which will take you closer to achieving your goal.
2. Carry out a similar procedure in order to identify the *restraining forces* — those which prevent your attaining your goal.
3. For clarification, write down both sets of forces in diagrammatic form.
4. In order to identify those forces (both driving and restraining) which need particular consideration, rate each one on a 1 to 5 scale on which 5 is 'very important' and 1 is 'of little importance'. Complete this quickly with a minimum of discussion.
5. Identify those which need the most urgent action (those which score 3 or more), also those on which the group can work together most effectively.
6. Having studied the major driving and restraining forces, decide upon a plan of campaign and note down the agreed course of action to be taken. Ways need to be found to *decrease* restraining forces and to *increase* and *strengthen* driving forces.

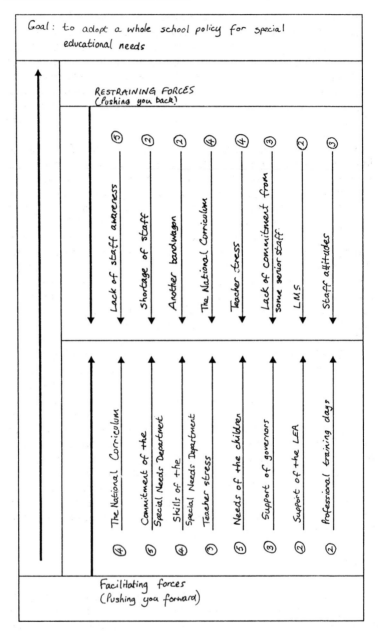

Figure 1.2 An example of force field analysis

The force field concept has been found to be particularly helpful in problem solving because it enables participants to consider the conflicting factors in a given situation. The force field demonstrates that the more we push or drive, the more likely it will be that resisting forces increase. The process of listening to and discussing the problems of those who are contributing to that resistance often has the effect of reducing the forces. This, in turn, will strengthen the driving forces thus promoting movement towards the ultimate goal.

Where an item appears both as a driving force and as a resisting force, it is worthwhile attempting to deal with both forces at the same time. Weigh up the pros and cons, then try to formulate a unified strategy. For example, *teacher stress* appears in figure 1.2 in both areas. It appears as a driving force because the adoption of appropriate learning strategies geared to pupils' special needs will encourage them to have more positive attitudes to teachers, thereby helping to reduce teachers' stress levels. On the other hand, *teacher stress* also occurs as a resisting force because some staff, who face the prospect of a more active role in dealing with special needs than previously, have expressed their qualms. One strategy for attempting to reconcile these conflicting forces might be through the medium of a professional training day for the staff concerned.

'No matter how serious or stressful the first encounter with a problem may seem, it is only a symptom of the underlying trouble or real problems.' In support of his statement Pokras (1989) cites the *Iceberg (or 80/20) Rule*, 'No matter how large the tip of an iceberg seems, 80 per cent of it lies below the surface of the water'. In his logical approach to problem-solving Pokras exhorts readers to look for the root cause of a problem which, like the layers of ice on an iceberg, lies below the surface and is the pivotal reason that has been the cause of the problem in the first place. In addition to variants of Force Field Analysis, he describes several other problem-solving techniques such as Charting Unknowns, Chronological Problem Analysis and Repetitive Why Analysis. Although primarily geared to business communication, his ideas could equally well be applied to management in education.

Setting objectives

A goal (such as the one used in the example of Force Field Analysis) is a general statement of what the participants in the change programme intend to achieve. Objectives are concerned with the means whereby that goal is attained. They describe observable actions, or changes in behaviour, at important stages in proceeding towards it (see Ainscow and Tweddle, 1979). Because of their specific nature, objectives tend to be contentious. However, those which arise as a result of the force field analysis are more likely to gain general agreement because they have evolved from the ensuing discussion. Some of the basic objectives which can be drawn from the present example are:

1. to raise awareness and understanding of all staff with regard to children's special educational needs;
2. to appraise curricular provision for these pupils;
3. to prepare staff for a pro-active role in collaborative teaching through a series of workshop sessions and training days;
4. to gain the wholehearted support of senior staff.

These will give a foundation on which to build further objectives.

Managing change

As participants in the change process over a period of time, readers will already be used to drawing up sets of objectives. Once this process has been carried out, the next stages in the change programme begin to gather momentum. From this point onwards, it will be the quality of management that will determine whether or not the specific goal is achieved. Four major aspects of successful change management are:

Helping others to cope with change

Following the work of Adams *et al*. (1976) it has been suggested that, irrespective of whether the change is unexpected or planned, pleasant or devastating, a predictable cycle of feelings is triggered off in those who are involved:

Immobilisation this is an initial period of shock or numbness which prevents a person taking action or thinking in a rational way.

Minimisation this stage is, in effect, a psychological 'breathing space' during which the individual attempts to minimise, and in some instances even deny, the extent of the change.

Self-doubt as the reality of the change begins to dawn, a person can suffer feelings of inadequacy, helplessness or even depression.

Acceptance of reality there is a gradual acceptance of the change and efforts are made to come to terms with it.

Testing   at this stage, new ideas are generated or new behaviours experimented with in order to discover what it means to be in a new situation.

Search for meaning   at this stage, the person concerned is able to stand back and to review the change more objectively. There is reflection on its impact.

Internalisation   finally, the change has become incorporated into the usual patterns of behaviour; new routines and relationships have been accepted and are on a positive footing.

Support for colleagues and organisations undergoing this process is crucial. It can take the form of praise, encouragement, counselling or simply lending a sympathetic ear. Evidence shows that where organisations have encouraged a flexibility of attitude amongst their staff, they have been more successful in helping them to face up to change as compared with those that are more hidebound.

In situations where certain individuals are confirmed opponents of change, it is preferable to minimise their direct role in the change process, if that is at all possible. Even so, keep them fully informed, attempt to surround them with a majority who are coming to accept the situation. In this way, the persons concerned are more likely to retire gracefully without loss of face. They may even join the 'winning' side rather than become isolated.

Becoming an effective communicator

Too much secrecy associated with change creates suspicion and often leads to unnecessary confrontations. Evolve a system for transmitting information and views to all concerned. Confidence and trust are more likely to become established through open communication and frank discussions of difficulties. Adequate training of personnel is an important element in transmitting new information, developing new skills, ironing out snags and in preparing people for change.

Encouraging a team approach

Teamwork is essential in successful change, although individual contributions from team members are to be encouraged. Interpersonal relationships should be supportive rather than competitive, each member being made to feel that his or her contribution is worthwhile.

Sharing decision making

Early involvement in the formulation of change will go a long way towards reducing behavioural resistance. Providing that policies and objectives have been clearly defined, team involvement will be enhanced through giving members the opportunity to share in decision making. Heirs (1986) argues that, 'Careful and creative thought is a pre-requisite for effective action. An organisation's future success, therefore, depends on the quality of its collective mind and how well that mind is managed'.

There is consistent evidence which shows that organisations, such as schools, which encourage the perception of change as a natural, continuing process and as an opportunity-providing aspect of their existence are more likely to manage resistance to change effectively and to benefit as a result.

Coping with stress

The report by Travers and Cooper (1990) emphasised that teaching is near the top of the occupational league table for stress, constant changes (and lack of information about them) being one of the major causes of pressure to be identified in the study. More recently, the Health and Safety Commission (1990) recognised the potential health risks caused by high levels of occupational stress. Situations at school, such as those described in this chapter, can make people more vulnerable to the effects of stress. Especially when combined with personal or other health problems, their capacity to cope with pressures at work can become impaired.

High levels of occupational stress can result not only in the impaired performance of members of staff but also in the less than efficient functioning of a school or organisation. The Commission estimated that up to 10 per cent of the workforce experienced some form of disabling emotional or physical ill health related to occupational stress, and that as many as 30 per cent suffered from a 'fluctuating array' of minor psychological discomforts and physical ailments. Amongst the causes of high stress levels were: poor communication; conflicts with colleagues; unnecessary paper work; inefficient meetings, and (in the case of special needs staff) teaching low ability children in mixed ability classes.

In discussing human resources and special needs Bowers (1987) identifies eight stress components of particular significance to special needs teachers. Of these, *role erosion, role ambiguity* and *role overload* seem particularly apposite to this chapter. Role erosion occurs when somebody sees a job that he or she has built up under threat from change, often as part of the process of redefining and creating new roles. Role ambiguity causes stress because people are not clear about the expectations which others have of them. Role overload comes as the result of too many expectations!

None of this seems to be good news for teachers and schools who, in addition to coping with the pace of change dictated by forces outside the school, are attempting to effect changes in their present management system.

Everyone experiences stress as a normal and natural function of living. Stress is the bodily reaction that enables us to adapt to the changes in our environment and to survive. It results in the way in which we perceive potentially threatening events. These trigger off an immediate psychological response in our bodies. We prepare either to fight back or to flee — or simply freeze in impotent inaction because we cannot deal adequately with the situation confronting us. This could be a real threat such as avoiding a speeding car or a dog out of control, or an imagined one such as being fearful about a forthcoming event. Therefore, it is not the actual situation itself that causes the ill-effects of stress, but the way an individual reacts to it. What needs to be achieved is a *balance* between the demands of the environment and a person's ability to respond.

When it is well managed, stress can become an exciting challenge, that spur to action which is so essential for success at work or for fulfilment in our leisure activities. Prompted by recent events and recent major studies, stress management is quickly gaining a high profile in education.

Concomitant with planning any activity in which major organisational change is envisaged, it would therefore seem prudent to institute processes whereby high levels of stress can be monitored and controlled. Such initiatives should come at both personal and organisation levels:

Personal level

1. Become fully aware of the longer-term effects of stress and the ways in which the body reacts to them:

    — Physiological — muscle tension leading to aches in the neck, shoulders and back; severe headaches; insomnia; constant weariness; loss of appetite; digestive upsets; high blood pressure, and 'nervous' skin ailments.
    — Psychological — feelings of frustration, helplessness and low self-esteem; heightened anxiety and nervous tension; forgetfulness and an inability to concentrate; irritability and moodiness.

2. In everyday working practices, attempt to prioritise activities, distinguishing and dealing first with really important ones as distinct from those which are merely urgent. Learn the art of saying 'No!' as a first step to becoming a more effective time manager (see chapter 12).

3. Be cognisant of the fact that everyone, however busy, needs some time to him or herself each day. Identify leisure activities which you find relaxing — swimming, gardening, tapestry, bird watching, or whatever — and reserve some regular time to practise them. Take up some form of relaxation programme, therapy or meditation (see Hewitt 1985, Powell 1988).

4. Adopt a simple relaxation technique which can be used easily when under stress.

Organisational level

1. Senior staff will need to recognise that high levels of occupational stress are harmful to colleagues and that the need to develop a supportive ethos in school is a real one.

2. All members of staff should recognise that reaction to undue stress is not a weakness and that those who suffer from it need sympathetic, sensitive support.

3. Establish an on-going staff training programme for stress management (the local School/Child Psychology Service can be helpful with this).

4. Train some senior members of staff as stress counsellors.

5. Encourage members of staff to identify informally a friend and colleague with whom they can discuss stressful situations and be sure of a supportive and sympathetic hearing.

6. Improve whole-staff debate and participation in the process of problem solving.

7. Reduce time pressures where possible. Set realistic deadlines and promote effective time management (see Chapter 12).

8. Encourage the LEA to adopt a policy for stress management.

In conclusion

One of the important uses of a change programme is to convert a frozen organisation into a flexible organisation. In the face of modern developments in education, schools have, of necessity, had to become more flexible in their outlook. This chapter has considered some of the aspects of change which need to be addressed in order that the process progresses smoothly and without high levels of occupational stress. Gone are the days of the 'hero innovator', the one-man-band or the member of staff whose admission of problems was taken as an indication of failure. Effective team-work has become the key to effective change — and personal survival.

References and further reading

Adams, J.D., Hayes, J. and Hopson, B. (1976) *Transition: Understanding and Managing Personal Change*, London: Martin Robertson.

Ainscow, M. and Tweddle, D. (1979) *Preventing Classroom Failure*, London: John Wiley.

Bowers, T. (1987) *Special Education Needs and Human Resource Management*, London: Croom Helm.

Brennan, W.K. (1979) *Curricular Needs of Slow Learners*, Schools Council Working Paper 63, London: Evans/Methuen.

DES (1978) *Special Educational Needs* (The Warnock Report), London: HMSO.

DES (1981) *Education Act*, London: HMSO.

DES (1988) *Education Reform Act*, London: HMSO.

Griffiths, D.E. (1975) 'Administrative theory and change in organisations' in Houghton, V. *et al.* (eds.) Management in Education Reader 1, *The Management of Organisations and Individuals*, London: Ward Lock/OU.

Health and Safety Commission (1990) *Managing Occupational Stress: A Guide for Managers and Teachers in the School Sector*, London: HMSO.

Heirs, B. with Farrell, P. (1986) *The Professional Decision Thinker*, London: Sidgwick and Jackson.

Hewitt, J. (1985) *Teach Yourself Relaxation*, Sevenoaks: Hodder and Stoughton.

Lewin, K. (1935) *A Dynamic Theory of Personality*, New York: McGraw.

Lewin, K. (1947) 'Frontiers in group dynamics' in *Human Relations*, 1.

Plant, R. (1987) *Managing Change — and Making It Stick*, Aldershot: Gower.

Pokras, S. (1989) *Systematic Problem Solving and Decision Making*, London: Kogan Page.

Powell, K. (1988) *Stress in Your Life*, Wellingborough: Thorsons.

Rawlinson, J.G. (1981) *Creative Thinking and Brainstorming*, Farnborough: Gower.

Reddin, W.J. (1970) 'Managing organisational change' in *Industrial Training International*, 5, 3.

Robson, C. and Wright, M. (1989) 'SEN: towards a modular pattern of INSET' in *Support for Learning*, 4, 2.

Stewart (1983) *Change: The Challenge for Management*, London: McGraw Hill.

Travers, C. and Cooper, C. (1990) *Survey on Occupational Stress Among Teachers in the United Kingdom*. Manchester University Institute of Science and Technology (for the NAS/UWT).

Part II
Assessment

2 National Curriculum delivery and assessment, the lessons of the first two years: an overview

Stewart Bourne

This chapter is intended to fulfil the following three broad objectives:

— to state the defining characteristics of the National Curriculum and its assessment arrangements;
— to consider how the above is working out in practice, at both school and classroom levels;
— to examine the implications of the National Curriculum implementation, delivery, assessment, record-keeping and reporting for the special needs child and his or her teacher within the mainstream classroom.

The nature of the beast

The content of this chapter is based upon the direct experience of the author within a wide variety of schools and classroom situations.

Much of the content applies to pupils of all levels of achievement although there is an emphasis upon the special needs child. For the purposes of this chapter, the notion of 'special needs' is given the widest possible interpretation and is taken to include all pupils who, for a variety of possible reasons, may be considered problematical in terms of teaching and learning.

The perception, if not the actual nature, of the teaching and learning process is being directly affected by the implementation of National Curriculum, sometimes in subtle and indirect ways, often in substantial and direct ways. Before embarking on a more detailed analysis of such changes and their implications for those pupils exhibiting learning difficulties, it is necessary to set the context within which this is happening and the beliefs and assumptions upon which it is based.

The National Curriculum, as a large-scale, centrally directed initiative, differs in several significant ways from previous attempts to direct or influence the curriculum 'diet' of pupils within state schools. The defining characteristics of the National Curriculum may be described as follows:

1. It is legislative in nature
   National Curriculum does not seek to initiate change by argument or persuasion but through the edict of law.
2. It is comprehensive in scope
   Many previous initiatives have often sought to direct or influence single aspects of teaching and learning such as curriculum content, the teaching and learning process itself and/or the observable outcomes of teaching and learning. National Curriculum attempts to address all of these factors and elements as a unified whole.
3. It is assessment-led
   National Curriculum may be described as assessment-led for at least three fundamental reasons,

   — the central role of assessment as the mechanism by which progress and achievement are defined, detected, monitored, evaluated and made available to a variety of audiences;

   — the description of the curriculum in terms of outcomes or objectives rather than content or general aims. Assessment must, by definition, assume a central role in any aspect of teaching and learning in which achievement has been pre-specified in the form of such outcomes or objectives;

— the assessment of achievement within the National Curriculum is, itself, viewed as an independent variable in the fostering of such achievement in the first place. In other words, assessment is viewed as the 'engine' which will both directly and indirectly improve the success rate of all pupils across a range of attainments.

It must be remembered, however, that whilst the structure and parameters of the National Curriculum may exist as statute, their interpretation and application are part of a dynamic process. In common with all processes involving both the interpretation of requirements and their application in a variety of different contexts and situations, the National Curriculum may manifest itself in very different ways and at a variety of levels. We may thus argue that, at classroom level, the interpretation and application of National Curriculum is not a uniform and standard process. National Curriculum implementation is the result of an ongoing and variable process, informed by the assumptions and beliefs of those involved and the pressures and changing priorities of the political and organisational structures in which it takes place.

Competing perspectives

The intended purpose of this chapter is a consideration of the assessment arrangements for the National Curriculum as they affect teachers and taught, rather than a theoretical discussion on the sociology of educational change. The author however makes no apology for raising certain points and issues which may be perceived as falling within this area. The speed with which the National Curriculum has been implemented and the pressure upon the classroom teacher to implement major changes, in an often unrealistic timescale, has resulted in significant areas of ambiguity, the clarification of which is open to competition. The author would contend that there is no shortage of groups and individuals more than willing 'to assist in this clarification process' for a variety of reasons and motivations. For the preceding reasons, it is vital that those involved with pupils at classroom level have a clear understanding of the process in which they are involved, and are able to exert a major influence upon the interpretation and implementation of the National Curriculum at the level of actual practice. It may be further argued that such an influence can only be brought about by an active understanding and involvement at the level of the ideas, beliefs and assumptions upon which actual classroom practice is based, or at the very least rationalised. It is only through such an understanding of both theory and practicalities that the teachers can seek to influence the process of National Curriculum implementation in ways that enhance both the learning experience and the actual achievements of the pupils for whom they are responsible.

Whatever happened to the TGAT Report?

We have argued that, for a variety of reasons, the National Curriculum may be described as assessment-led. It may be useful to consider the advent of the National Curriculum in terms of those first principles of assessment purposes and practice proposed within the report by the Task Group for Assessment and Testing (TGAT). Many would argue that such first principles have either been forgotten or changed out of all recognition — 'Nobody talks about TGAT now'. It may, however, be argued that the TGAT principles have not been forgotten, or even altered, but that their various elements have undergone changes of priority resulting from a mixture of political and practical considerations and pressures. The TGAT report outlined four major functions of assessment:

— *Formative* That the information gained from the assessment process should be used to plan for the progress of both the individual and groups of pupils through the taught curriculum.
— *Diagnostic* That the information gained from the assessment process should be used to identify individual learning needs and/or difficulties in order that appropriate and thus effective action may be taken.
— *Summative* That, at appropriate points, the achievements of an individual pupil should be brought together, reflected upon, and reported to various audiences.
— *Evaluative* That the data gained from the assessment process should be used to evaluate the effectiveness of the teaching and learning process at a variety of levels and within a variety of contexts.

Of course, all of the aforementioned aspects of functions of assessment existed prior to the advent of National Curriculum, particularly within the special needs sector. What we must constantly remind ourselves, however, is that we are not just discussing assessment in general, as some sort of global principle, but rather the assessment of achievement within a prescribed curriculum. Furthermore this curriculum is described in terms of objectives or targets, the attainment of which is seen to constitute achievement. It was generally agreed that, with some reservations, the TGAT principles were 'ideologically sound'; most of the reservations were related to either the principle of an objectives-led National Curriculum or those functions of assessment described as evaluative. Most teachers would argue that the formative and diagnostic functions of assessment are central to good practice regardless of the nature or content of the desired outcomes in curriculum terms. Most would agree that there is a need to summarise a pupil's achievements at various points in time in order to inform parents/guardians and other involved parties, not least the pupil, of current progress and possible ways forward. Many, including the author, have deep reservations about the manner in which the evaluative function of assessment has been interpreted and its increasing priority as perhaps the dominant function of assessment in terms of its effect upon the teacher, the pupil, and the school within which they come together. These points will be explored at a greater depth within the next section, which concentrates on the current position of the classroom teacher.

Problems of belief, practice and perspective

The experience of the last two years has demonstrated that the pressures arising from the very nature and context of National Curriculum assessment arrangements at classroom level, have often resulted in some justifiable confusion and stress on the part of the teacher. Such confusion and stress are often particularly apparent where the following circumstances apply:

1. that the teacher is attempting to both deliver and assess certain elements of the curriculum that are unfamiliar in content and process;
2. that the teacher is either confused about, or philosophically opposed to, the relationship of assessment to the taught curriculum, the child and the methods by which progress has been previously measured;
3. that the teacher is either confused about, or philosophically opposed to, a system of assessment that is criterion-referenced, rather than normative, in nature;
4. that the teacher has some difficulty in interpreting the actual requirements of the assessment process, particularly those involving:

   — the interpretation of attainment targets/statements of attainment,
   — the formulation of practical assessment criteria,

— the nature and purpose of 'evidence',
— the role of record-keeping,
— an externally moderated element in the form of standard assessment tasks;

5. that the teacher believes that the implementation of National Curriculum, particularly those elements relating to assessment, will result in unacceptable changes to teaching methods, classroom relationships and desirable educational outcomes;
6. that the teacher believes that the needs of those pupils experiencing learning difficulties would either not be met or assume a lower priority under National Curriculum pressures;
7. that the levels and quality of support and training, both within and without the school are not sufficient to meet the teacher's needs;
8. that the workload involved is both prohibitive and detrimental to the delivery of good practice within the classroom.

The above list is not exhaustive but does express some of those major concerns most frequently expressed by those classroom teachers directly involved in National Curriculum implementation, particularly within the primary phase.

National Curriculum and the classroom teacher

A central objective of this chapter is an attempt to assist the classroom teacher in gaining an overall view or perspective of National Curriculum requirements. Such an overall view is essential in the formulation of the informed professional stance necessary to influence the processes by which National Curriculum requirements will be evaluated and modified during the years of implementation. Experience has also demonstrated that such an overall perspective is equally essential for the implementation of National Curriculum within the classroom, in ways that support and enhance existing good practice.

One way of exploring National Curriculum assessment issues at a practical level is to take some of the areas which classroom teachers have identified as major problems and/or concerns and consider these in the light of experience. It must be stated, however, that experience has demonstrated that a close relationship exists between the perception of difficulties by the classroom teacher and particular interpretations of National Curriculum requirements, especially the exact relationship between assessment, curriculum delivery and the identification of achievement and/or learning difficulties.

Some 'wit' once compared the English educational system to the rediscovery of the Americas by Christopher Columbus, 'He didn't know where he was going when he set out, he didn't know where he was when he arrived and he didn't know where he had been when he got back'. A more accurate and fairer analogy would be that there is a multiplicity of passionately held views concerning where we should be going and how we will know when we have arrived. Since the National Curriculum attempts to decide all of these things on our behalf, it is natural that our perceptions of both the problems and opportunities, presented by the National Curriculum will be largely determined by our own personal philosophy concerning the desirable outcomes of education. It is essential that when we are confronted with particular aspects or elements of National Curriculum that we find highly problematical we examine our own beliefs and assumptions in an equally critical way in order accurately to define the nature of the problem.

Many teachers, particularly within the primary sector, are used to an essentially content-led curriculum. In practical terms this has meant that, in planning the curriculum, decisions have initially been taken concerning the subject matter of the teaching often expressed in terms of cross-curricular 'topics or projects'. Once the subject matter has been decided upon, then learning opportunities for particular skills of numeracy, literacy and other areas have been identified and planning for actual delivery undertaken. Decisions about the assessment of progress and achievement may well not have been specified at this point or have been of a very generalised nature. Pupils exhibiting special needs in the widest sense may have been given specific experiences, practice or relevant tasks depending on their designated difficulties. This is of course a gross oversimplification of the process but is intended to illustrate a particular approach. When faced with the demands of National Curriculum many teachers well-versed in the previously described approach have experienced understandable difficulties.

Much National Curriculum related in-service training has sought to reassure teachers by arguing that 'this is nothing really new and, at most, constitutes a few extra planning tasks and a little tightening-up on the assessment front'. Such training has often taken the form of the production of a traditional content-based topic or project web from which opportunities for the delivery and assessment of National Curriculum statements of attainment/attainment targets have been subsequently identified. Many teachers have, in the light of experience, come to realise that this is something very new and that the attempt to graft new demands on top of existing practices is, however worthy, almost impossible.

National Curriculum and the objectives-led approach

As we have argued earlier, National Curriculum is best understood as essentially objectives- and not content-led. In practical terms, this means that decisions concerning what a child shall know, understand and be able to do as a result of experiencing the curriculum have been taken beforehand and expressed in terms of statements of attainment/attainment targets. The learning experience, expressed as programmes of study and general content or subject matter, is intended primarily to service these objectives or outcomes. Assessment is intended to identify the attainment of these objectives and outcomes by the pupil, establish acceptable progress in terms of such attainment, identify difficulties that may be preventing acceptable progress and inform the planning of curriculum delivery so as to maximise effectiveness in terms of pupil progress. It follows from this that assessment is:

— *criterion-referenced* — the criteria provided by the statement of attainment/attainment targets
— *formative and diagnostic* — in that planning for progress and the identification of difficulties are the direct result of the assessment process
— *summative* — in that there is a common 'yardstick' against which progress and achievement may be summarised and reported
— *evaluative* — in that the effectiveness of teaching and learning may be evaluated against common criteria.

The author is not making an argument for or against the principles upon which National Curriculum is based but, rather, attempting to highlight the fact that, in both content and process, it differs significantly from previous practice, particular within the primary sector. These differences have particular implications for the way that planning is undertaken and the type of support required by the teacher in terms of both training and whole school policy and practice and it is essential that they are understood in their totality by all concerned.

National Curriculum and the special needs pupil

We have attempted to clarify the nature of the intended relationship between the curriculum, the pupil and the teacher in terms of National Curriculum assessment. We have not, as yet, specifically discussed the context of the special needs pupil within this process.

The reason for this is important, quite simply the points under discussion apply equally to *all* pupils experiencing the National Curriculum and to the many teachers attempting to deliver it. The special needs pupil will, in the majority of cases, remain a National Curriculum pupil enjoying, in statutory terms, an equal entitlement. The teacher cannot deliver this entitlement and utilise his or her skills to enhance the opportunities of the special needs pupil until the demands of the National Curriculum itself are clearly understood.

The model for National Curriculum delivery and assessment discussed within this chapter is fine in theory but demands closer examination in terms of the experience of the last two years, especially those aspects that have presented teachers with particular difficulties. It is certainly true that some teachers do not accept the principles underlying any system of criterion-referenced assessment and remain convinced that the quality and nature of the information gained through a directly comparative or normative approach is of greater value in determining the relative progress of individual pupils. This belief does not usually result from a desire to rank-order pupils as a ready indication of ability, but rather a desire to relate progress to the particular circumstances and situations of the pupils concerned.

> 'None of my poor little souls will ever reach Level 2 this year and it seems so unfair to have to keep assessing and reporting the fact, as well as a waste of time.'
>
> 'There is such a massive gap between Level 1 and Level 2 but it won't look much when mum and dad get the report, they'll wonder what the child has been doing for two years.'

Once again it can be argued that this viewpoint either results from a fundamental disagreement with the basic tenets of National Curriculum assessment or a misunderstanding of their intended functions. An important element of these functions is to locate precisely the attainment of pupils on a common national scale, regardless of individual or group circumstances. When expressed in terms of crude National Curriculum levels, this can appear grossly unfair to the various participants. It seems unfair to the child because it appears to belittle great feats of individual progress within broad levels of attainment. It appears unfair to the hard-pressed teacher because it seems to belittle herculean efforts on his or her part for relatively small amounts of progress on the child's part. The final level of apparent unfairness concerns the school itself which may, given the particular circumstances of its location and intake, be open to uninformed, simplistic and negative comparisons with other more privileged institutions. There are no comfortable answers to these deeply felt concerns, but there are points which can be advanced to move the argument forward, or at least clarify it a little.

— There is a generally held and powerful belief, within both educational circles and the wider public arena, that there exists a need for national criteria against which the educational progress of pupils may be measured and evaluated at significant points in their school career.
— Normative-referenced systems cannot, in themselves, provide such nationally accepted criteria. Witness the current, rather sterile debate about reading standards, where the various protagonists base their arguments upon differing assumptions and ground rules concerning what constitutes reading ability, or the lack of it, and how you recognise it in the first place.
— Arguments and/or concerns about the fairness, applicability or relevance of particular national criteria must be clearly separated from arguments about the desirability of establishing criteria in the first place which are probably, given the intentions of all the major political parties, a lost cause anyway.
— Properly applied systems of criterion-referenced assessment supporting well-designed, objectives-led curriculum innovations have tended to enhance the achievements of all pupils, particularly those viewed as potentially low-attaining.
— If the need arises, the information gained through criterion-referenced systems of assessment may be used in a normative way; in fact it is precisely this point that is concerning many teachers who feel that rank-ordered data will be used to make invidious comparisons between schools.

Thus, we may almost certainly assume that, although the nature of the criteria may change over time, we will be working with a system of national attainment targets serviced within school by various forms of criterion-referenced assessment.

The lessons of experience

If the above points are accepted we are still left with some major problems and issues that require practical resolution and it is at this point that we may draw upon practical experience. Even those teachers philosophically committed to an objectives-led approach, serviced through criterion-referenced assessment, have found difficulties with the attendant workload. It would be most useful at this point to highlight the major areas of difficulty and provide examples of those approaches and practices which appear to have been most effective.

Because of the way in which National Curriculum is structured the teacher is faced with a fourfold problem in order to facilitate learning best. These involve decisions about: what exactly is to be delivered in terms of actual teaching content; how this is best planned; how achievement will be recognised in terms of assessment; and what are the most effective methods of recording progress. Decisions about actual content can only be reached on the basis of a thorough understanding of the attainment targets/ statements of attainment within the context of the programmes of study that support them. Neither programmes of study nor attainment targets/statements of attainment are a recipe for teaching methods, which remain firmly within the professional autonomy of the classroom teacher. The former are an attempt to describe a certain minimum coverage of content, experiences, knowledge, skills and understanding that will need to be undergone, practised and acquired in order to facilitate the achievement of the latter. They attempt to describe the 'what' without dictating the 'how'. We must remind ourselves that the programmes of study and their associated attainment targets/statements of attainment constitute a statutory entitlement for all pupils to whom they apply. This problem of interpretation constitutes the first function of in-school moderation.

Experience has clearly demonstrated that this task of interpretation is best undertaken, either formally or informally, by small groups of teachers supported through the effective and sympathetic use of directed time and other whole-school arrangements. A teacher working alone, whatever the quality of in-service training and nonstatutory guidelines, faces a daunting and unnecessarily burdensome task. The fact that this process of interpretation is necessary is indisputable given the somewhat vague manner in which certain statements of attainment are expressed and the need to formulate suitable assessment criteria. Teachers' approaches to planning have generally fallen into two broad categories which at their respective extremes may be stated as, 'We do our own thing and fit the National Curriculum into it', or 'We do the National Curriculum and fit our own thing into it'. The former approach has usually taken the form of planning and forecasting desirable curriculum coverage, without direct reference to National Curriculum requirements, and then auditing this to see where National Curriculum teaching opportunities appear. The latter approach has taken programmes of study and attainment targets/statements of attainment as the starting point for planning and then identified opportunities for the inclusion of other, non-National Curriculum content and outcomes that are felt to be educationally desirable.

Putting aside more general arguments about the worthiness of each approach, it must be stated that those taking National Curriculum requirements as the starting point for curriculum planning have experienced fewer difficulties in terms of workload and assessment. This has been particularly true where a class contains special needs pupils in the widest sense of the term. Enhancing the opportunities of such pupils has always demanded some fairly rigorous planning and never more so than when the content and intended outcomes of the curriculum may, in parts, be unfamiliar to the teacher. Most of us with experience of teaching special needs pupils within the mainstream classroom are aware that little can be left to chance.

The context of assessment

When working to interpret the requirements of programmes of study and attainment targets/statements of attainment for the purposes of curriculum delivery, initial decisions about both assessment and record-keeping must also be made. It is at this point that the nature and purpose of National Curriculum assessment need to be explicitly understood and the opportunities and difficulties viewed within a practical context. This is the area that has caused the most difficulty for many teachers and is partly the result of the systematic undermining of people's confidence in their own professional skills and autonomy. This has come about through both the imposition of a curriculum over which they perceive themselves as having little control and the general targeting as being single-handedly responsible for the decline of western civilisation. Ironically, it is precisely at this point that the demands upon the skills and professionalism of the teacher are greatest. The success of National Curriculum, as a mechanism for enhancing opportunity and achievement, relies totally upon the considered application of assessment techniques in ways that can only be achieved when mediated and practised through the skills of the classroom teacher.

We must once again remind ourselves that National Curriculum assessment is the assessment of pupil performance against a taught curriculum, the outcomes of which are stated in terms of attainment targets/statements of attainment. In planning for the actual delivery of curriculum content, decisions must be taken concerning evidence of attainment. The term evidence of attainment may, in most circumstances, be viewed as interchangeable with assessment criteria. In other words, what must the pupil do to convince the teacher that a particular skill, aspect of knowledge or understanding has been acquired? This task is not as simple or straightforward as it may appear. It may often be difficult, and is usually inappropriate, to base such a judgment upon a single, or even series of pre-determined tasks, especially where the lower attaining pupil is concerned.

A common criticism made by classroom teachers of criterion-referenced assessment concerns the 'shelf-life' of any judgments made. There is an understandable reluctance to commit oneself to specific judgments about a pupil's learning when he or she may not be able to demonstrate the same competence in a week's time. In many ways, it is more comfortable to record and report that Janet is in the top 10 per cent of her class for mathematics, backed up with a few generalised statements about the kind of work that she has undertaken and any major difficulties and/or successes experienced. It can be a less comfortable experience when we are required to convince ourselves professionally that Janet has definitely mastered the skills of data handling, as expressed in a national statement of attainment, and then be required to record and report the fact for public and professional scrutiny.

The teacher as assessor

For the variety of reasons previously mentioned within this chapter, many teachers see themselves as the subject of professional and public scrutiny based upon a new model of individual and organisa-tional accountability. The effects of changing perceptions of accountability have been particularly apparent within the mainstream primary sector. This situation has sometimes resulted in a reluctance, on the part of teachers, to make specific judgments on pupil progress against National Curriculum statements of attainment without some form of external validation. Given the previously described situation, there is a very natural temptation to place judgments upon progress within a context of external objective proof, the main purpose of which is to convince people, other than the teachers themselves, that learning has indeed taken place, or, was at least evident when the child was assessed. This approach is intended somehow to externalise judgments by making the teacher an objective and dispassionate coordinator of the assessment process in ways that are more akin to the examiner and may, for the reasons outlined, be initially attractive. This approach will often take the form of designing a tight set of tasks, worksheets and/or tests, the successful completion of which can be taken as proof of achievement. This situation will also frequently result in the retention and storage of large quantities of pupil output in the form of written work, projects or artifacts which are also intended to service the perceived burden of proof.

Whilst the situation described within the previous paragraph is understandable, it is, in the author's opinion, detrimental to both teacher and pupil, particularly the special needs pupil who stands every chance of becoming marginalised within the whole process. The teacher who either feels the need, or is pressurised into adopting the 'examiner's' approach, will have all his worst suspicions about 'assessment' duly confirmed; that it constitutes an extra and alien burden of work, undertaken for unacceptable or obscure reasons and interferes with the prime task of teaching children. It is detrimental to the pupil because it changes the nature of the professional relationship between teacher and taught in ways that may affect all pupils, but will certainly affect the special needs pupil through a constant identification of difficulty without the time and opportunity to remedy the situation. All pupils will, in most circumstances, be following a common curriculum, their progress against the outcomes or objectives of which not only has to be assessed, monitored and recorded by the teacher but, by its very nature and intent, is open to public scrutiny. Given this situation the dangers to the education of the special needs child within a mainstream classroom, with the best will in the world, are readily apparent. The special needs pupils is, and must remain, what the name implies, a child requiring and deserving special attention in the form of planning, teaching, assessment and recording in order to foster and maintain progress. Any approach to teaching and assessment which ignores this fact is not only unfair but ineffective.

Teacher as professional v. the 'Examiner's' approach to assessment

At its best, the National Curriculum and its assessment arrangements are intended to constitute a statutory entitlement for all pupils within the state system that will pursue common standards, foster achievement and guarantee equality of provision, in curriculum, if not material terms. The author believes that, given certain circumstances, this can indeed be achieved but that significant factors may militate against such success. One such circumstance is the 'examiner's' approach to assessment described above. The essence of useful and effective National Curriculum assessment is that, rather than being removed from the process, the teacher remains central and is the very medium through which professionally informed judgments are both made and respected. We may, for the purposes of this chapter, call this the 'teacher as professional' approach to assessment to distinguish it from the 'examiner's' approach previously described. This approach is based upon a difference in perception and seeks to reinforce the view of the classroom teacher as a skilled practitioner, who selects and uses the information gained from the assessment process to inform professional decision-making as part of a continuous process, and not as a substitute for it.

It was stated at the beginning of this chapter that the original report by the Task Group for Assessment and Testing took an approach to assessment that was generally considered both to be sound and reflect notions of good practice. It was also argued that, under a variety of pressures, the emphasis has changed somewhat resulting in a concentration upon the summative and evaluative aspects of assessment at the possible expense of the formative and diagnostic. Everyone concerned will deny this vehemently but these are the 'hidden' messages that the classroom teacher has received from 'on high', and what people believe to be real will be real in its consequences. The 'teacher as professional' approach to assessment requires a measure of political and public confidence in the teaching body which is not always apparent, but most of all it requires an act of professional assertion by teachers who will need to take the initiative, regardless of the pressures.

From this perspective, the teacher's prime concern is with the formative and diagnostic aspects of assessment as an inseparable component of the teaching process itself. The overall context remains the same, the assessment of pupil progress against the objectives or outcomes of a taught National Curriculum to which pupils enjoy a statutory entitlement. Planning remains equally rigorous; for the reasons outlined earlier little happens by chance, particularly where the special needs child is involved. Assessment is viewed as integral to teaching in that it informs decisions rather than merely describing progress. This may operate at a variety of levels, if a teacher observes a child having difficulties with a task or activity, intervenes and provides support and guidance which enables the child to progress with that task or activity, he or she has undertaken an act of formative assessment. If a teacher, in considering the overall success of a group of pupils against a National Curriculum statement of attainment, decides that the particular skill, understanding or area of knowledge is not being acquired to an acceptable degree and needs 're-visiting' with a change of approach, he has undertaken an act of formative assessment. If, as a result of the assessment and monitoring of reading progress for an individual pupil, it becomes apparent that certain difficulties are being experienced that may, or may not, fall within the competence of the classroom teacher to remedy, he or she has been involved in an act of diagnostic assessment.

The major difference in this approach is that the decisions are not inherent within the assessment itself, but within the professional decisions taken, informed by the collection and interpretation of the information gained from assessment. Evidence of attainment becomes, not the required 'proof' for the purposes of scrutiny by some third party, but the basis upon which a teacher assesses the progress of individual and/or groups of pupils. The actual assessment will take many forms, both formal and informal, planned and occurring spontaneously as opportunities and situations unfold. The main point is that whatever is happening is, and must be, mediated, judged and appraised by the teacher. None of this conflicts with the requirements of National Curriculum delivery and/or assessment, it is rather a question of emphasis.

Standard assessment tasks

We have not discussed the evolving role and context of standard assessment tasks, to which another chapter could easily be dedicated. Again, much depends upon the perspective from which they are approached, 'teacher as examiner' or 'teacher as professional'. As a profession we must evaluate standard assessment tasks by the quality and usefulness of the information they provide in relation to the time, effort and costs, both overt and hidden, involved in their application. If the information gained is genuinely useful in assisting the teacher to make the type of professional decision required to foster and maintain pupil progress then it is a useful and valid exercise, if not, then a waste of scarce resources, not least time. As with many aspects of National Curriculum, standard assessment tasks may be attempting to serve too many purposes, some of them contradictory or even mutually exclusive.

Conclusions

In conclusion, and on the basis of actual experience, we may advance some provisional criteria for effectiveness in the delivery and assessment of National Curriculum with the special needs pupil, and arguably, all pupils.

Teaching and learning within the National Curriculum appears to be most effective when:

— the teacher involved both understands and is sympathetic towards the practice and principles of criterion-referenced assessment;

— the teacher involved believes that the organisation of teaching and learning is of greater influence on pupil progress than considerations of 'innate ability' or 'social and economic deprivation';

— National Curriculum is perceived, for planning, delivery and assessment purposes as objectives-led, rather than content-led;

— the interpretation of teaching requirements, in terms of programmes of study, statements of attainment and attainment targets, is undertaken collectively and supported by a strong collective moderation process;

— the formulation of assessment criteria, against which evidence of attainment may be sought and evaluated, is undertaken collectively and supported by a strong collective moderation process;

— the teacher regards him or herself as the professional, whose skills are central to initiation, management and interpretation of the learning process, particularly those elements involving the assessment and evaluation of pupil progress;

— pupils understand exactly what is expected of them in terms of learning and are given a variety of opportunities to demonstrate positive and progressive achievement however, apparently, limited such progress may appear;

— the processes of teaching and learning within the National Curriculum are supported by an effective system of record-keeping, which is both practicable and genuinely useful to the teacher in making professional judgments and decisions;

— parents/guardians are involved, wherever possible and in a variety of ways, in the support of teaching and learning;

— all of the above factors are fostered and supported through clear, sympathetic and effective whole-school policy, which is itself open to regular evaluation and review involving those whose efforts it seeks to support.

3 Personalising the whole-school policy

Joseph Winterbourne

Introduction

Anyone returning to school after a career break or moving from one
branch of education to another is struck immediately by the huge
increase in written policy documents that schools have published.
These are especially noticeable in terms of whole-school policies. As
schools have come to terms with their changing obligations and as
a response to the practical implications of accountability, they have
contrived to produce effective written statements. These are
extremely important in enabling schools to meet their legal obligations and in setting benchmarks against which a school's progress
can be evaluated. Such whole-school policies as *equal opportunities,
special educational needs, health and safety, assessment recording and
reporting* and so on have now become familiar titles in staff hand-
books and familiar areas of questioning in interviews. However the
development and publication of whole-school policies are not ends
in themselves. They have to be more than a statement of the school's
responses to the 1981 and 1988 Education Acts. At a time of LMS
and real difficulties in maintaining funding, it is easy for schools to
pay lip service to special educational needs by pointing to a policy
document and a coordinator. For a whole-school policy to work it
has to be able to relate to individual pupils. It is against this
background that I wish to discuss some procedures for helping with
the implementation of a whole-school policy on special educational
needs.

Identification

The introduction of the National Curriculum should greatly assist teachers in the identification of children's special educational needs. However I do not believe that it will do the coordinator's job for them. Most schools still concur with the general findings of the Warnock Report, that at any one time some 20 per cent of pupils will be experiencing special educational needs, as an accurate working guideline. The fact that this is not a fixed amount nor a fixed population means that schools must constantly reassess those pupils it feels have special educational needs. The initial stage in the identification of special needs will have occurred in the primary schools. Although using differing criteria and procedures, each section of infant and primary schooling will have identified for its own needs those pupils who are experiencing difficulties significantly greater than the majority of their peers. This information will increasingly be part of the pupil's record.

Curriculum continuity

The transfer to senior school will involve close liaison with Year 6 teachers which will allow pupils' needs and strengths to be fully discussed so that subject teachers in senior schools can successfully build on the National Curriculum levels already achieved. Each school must devise suitable procedures to capture the wealth of information that is available. In the current state of uncertainty concerning the accuracy or otherwise of SATs, there is no substitute for face-to-face discussions. This inevitably means using a great deal of time. Primary colleagues are dependent on the goodwill of their headteachers or deputies to release them for discussions. In the senior school, time to visit has to be made from the time due to Year 11 students going on study leave. Of equal importance is the ability to transmit this information successfully to colleagues. Eventually, as staff collectively become more familiar with attainment targets in a variety of subjects it may be possible to discuss pupils' needs meaningfully in National Curriculum jargon without it being part of a new mystification process.

Figure 3.1 shows part of a summary sheet that is used to collate information beyond the bare bones of National Curriculum levels. The complexity of National Curriculum reporting tends to make it too unwieldy to have a summary sheet that would have every piece of information about every child on it. The sheet is used to gain an overview of pupils in each feeder school. The categories included can be as wide or narrow as the individual school wishes in order to suit its pastoral policy for class organisation. In this case, the information required is seen as a support to any National Curriculum evidence that is available since it deals with issues that have to be planned and dealt with in a whole-school manner. Disabilities may have a greater or lesser impact in a subject area but they are with the student all the time. Everyone needs this information as soon as possible in order to integrate it into their programmes of study. The key for figure 3.1 explains the headings used in greater detail. An important adjunct to this summary sheet is the examples of evidence and their context that will increasingly be part of the pupil's record. From a special needs point of view a piece of free writing which has not had the benefit of redrafting is especially useful in gauging the skills mastered in presentation, spelling and language structures.

Transmitting information to colleagues

The information in figure 3.1 is used initially as a central resource by those staff involved in planning the special educational needs support in the school. It is used to inform the groupings made by the pastoral head of lower school and also as the basis of discussions with subject areas to plan the provisions of support for the pupils. An opportunity needs to be found to transmit this information to the wide body of staff that are involved with the Year 7 pupils. However, because there is inevitably an adjustment between the initial comments from the feeder primary schools and the effect of the transition to senior school, it is not always suitable simply to dish out this information in the form of a list which takes on the appearance of something permanent. The best way of transmitting the information is to share all the relevant information with the pastoral and teaching staff in a series of short meetings at the beginning of the school year, or at the end of the summer term, if the timetable and groupings have been finalised.

Figure 3.2 allows the special needs coordinator to widen the scope for transmitting information by focusing on the individual subject teachers' responses to pupils once they have settled into their new school. The form can be used either to provide a snapshot of a whole new class allowing the use of some standardised tests or it can be used to record individual subject teachers' recommendations concerning children who are experiencing difficulties greater than the majority of their peers, or who are excelling in some or all subjects. The importance of the form is as an aid to identifying needs in preparation for providing and monitoring the provision being made. At this stage it is very useful to be able to provide subject staff with a clear idea of the general ability levels of the pupils. There is a need to be able to assess the reading levels both in terms of reading ages

NAMES	Disabilities	SEN	More Able	Low Achiever	Child Psy. Support	E2L	Reading	Support Materials used	COMMENT
Diana W	Profoundly deaf in both ears.	✓			Extra help from H.I.Serv. ✓		7.00.	General work. No set reading scheme used.	Absence is very high. Tends to forget / lose hearing aids.
Elizabeth R			✓				14.00	Has been working on project on Women in War to a challenge.	Very articulate, responds well. Some written structures need improving to make full use of potential.
David B	Clumsy child syndrome.		✓		Receiving regular physiotherapy.		13.8	Has been encouraged to use I.T. facilities.	David has very poor written presentation. Gives a very false impression of his abilities.
John F	Poor eyesight. Doesn't wear his glasses.	✓			Report available.		8.00	Fuzzbuzz scheme and phonic worksheets.	Very weak in all areas. See Educ. Psychologist's report.
Arthur S	Very bad asthma and eczema.	✓		✓			9.6		Very poor handwriting and very easily upset.
Wayne G	Spina Bifida. Speech problems.	✓			Has speech		8.9	Speech therapist will come in to give advice.	Can manage to climb stairs but can overbalance easily.
Sarah H			✓	Does no work.			16.00		Appears to be extremely clever. Family very worried as she does not complete any homework. Scores top marks in exams but only if it requires no extended writing.

Figure 3.1   Continuity year 6/7, special education needs, primary school

Key

Disabilities	this is usually used to indicate a physical or medical condition.
SEN	refers to pupils who are on the primary school special special educational needs register and may proceed to the senior school register.
More Able	this is used to identify pupils who have outstanding ability within the group but is not as restrictive as the term 'gifted pupil'.
Low Achiever	this category is used to alert staff to the group of children who appear to be significantly underachieving whatever their level.
Child Psy support	this indicates pupils who are on the Child Psychology Service register and should indicate that there is some sort of report available.
E2L	this stands for English as a second language and refers to pupils who have had an inadequate exposure to English usually because they are recent arrivals to the country.
Reading	this is used to capture any results or observations on the reading standards of the pupils.
H.I. Serv.	this refers to the Hearing Impaired Service.

Figure 3.1 (*cont*) Continuity year 6/7, special education needs, primary school

as supplied through tests and in terms of the readability of the text they will encounter. To do this in the current debate on reading is to invite criticism. Not to do it is to render a disservice to colleagues who are willing to use such information in a professional manner as part of the total picture being offered. In practical terms the gradual building up of a set of readability profiles based on the actual materials the pupils will be working with is probably the most useful since they will allow the special needs staff the most scope for using their expertise to help children access the curriculum fully. The forms have to be inter-active to be successful. Most colleagues can tell within a very short time which pupils are experiencing above average difficulties in their subjects, especially if they have already moved to a differentiated curriculum. However, very few subject departments have formulated a policy on what constitutes special educational needs in their subject areas. As this has important repercussions for assessment it is an area that departments will be forced to address sooner rather than later. Information is probably only as good as the use that is made of it. If the information available on figures 3.1 and 3.2 is used to inform the curriculum offered to pupils then genuine changes in methodology and resourcing are likely to take place. The context in which this information is given

NAMES	Junior Rec.	Junior R.A.	Yr.7 R.A.	Spell	AH2	Eng.	Math	Sc.	Tech	Hist	G	Mod Lang	PE	Art	Mus	Dr	PSE
Diana W	SEN	7.4	7.10	7.3	E	✿	✿	✿		✿	✿						✿
Elizabeth R	M.A.	16+	16+	16	A	✓	✓	✓	✓	✓	✓	✓	✓	✓	✓	✓	✓
David B	SEN	13.8	14.00	13.00	B	✓				✓							
John F K	SEN	8.00	8.2	7.8	E	✿	✿	✿			✿						
Arthur S	SEN	9.6	9.8	9.2	D						✿			✿			
Wayne F		11.2	11.4	10.8	C												
Sarah H	M.A.	16.00	16.00	16.00	A							✓		✓			
Nigel M	SEN	8.3	8.4	7.8	E	✿	✿	✿								✿	
Terry W		10.00	10.2	9.8	C												
Mohammed Y		11.6	10.4	10.8	C												
Abdul A	E2L																
Ashley W	M.A.	12.8	13.2	13.00	B	✓		✓				✓	✓			✓	
Tracey U		12.10	13.00	12.4	B		✓	✓									

Key

Junior Rec. this refers back to figure 3.1 and covers whether a child is on the SEN register is M.A. (more able)
             L.A. (Low Achiever).

Junior R.A. refers to any reading age that is available.

Yr 7 R.A.   refers to any standardised reading age score that is available.

Spell   refers to any standardised spelling score.
AH2   this refers to NFER AH2 test that is still used as part of the general identification procedures.

The rest of the columns refer to subjects.
✿   indicates there are special educational needs considerations.
✓   indicates subject agreement with More Able designation.

Figure 3.2 Classlist showing pupils with special educational needs

is important. Traditionally in schools, a divide exists between the pastoral and the academic roles that colleagues take on. For administrative purposes this is useful but for the students it can be counter-productive as their needs cannot be so neatly pigeon-holed. Therefore the best context is to give information as soon as possible at the start of the school year with feedback from individual teachers as soon as possible within the first half-term.

Individual statement of needs

Once individual children have been screened out, a more refined statement of their needs and the provision to be made can be negotiated with the individual subject teachers. Figure 3.3. shows such a statement allowing the provision to be matched to the subject needs and indicating, where possible, its relevance to other subject areas in which it might not be possible to provide direct support. The subject needs do not have to be restricted or couched in National Curriculum jargon. They should be entered in a manner which is as straightforward and least threatening as possible, especially in view of the fact that they may well be used to discuss the provision made and the progress of a pupil with his parents. This way of working is very labour-intensive, relying as it does on good liaison skills to ensure that provision is made by *somebody* not necessarily only by a special needs support teacher. This is more problematic than it sounds since identifying a student as having special educational needs can be interpreted by some colleagues as being someone else's problem. The reality is that the more everything is given a price the less resources will be directly available to any individual pupil.

Types of support

The type and amount of support to be offered to either an individual or a group of pupils is a very vexed question in the current debate on school resources and value for money. There is no single answer that will fit all situations. However there are some general points that seem to follow from the acceptance of a whole-school policy. The first is that it must be continuously stressed that special educational needs are *every* teacher's responsibility. Schools may develop preferred ways of utilising resources but the acceptance of a whole-school policy means that eventually every teacher will have to become more adept at delivering a differentiated curriculum to their pupils. At present this is assumed in any mixed ability arrangement.

Central to this whole question of provision is the ability to build in the flexibility to recognise that students' needs are not static and that they will vary across the curriculum. This is because the expertise of individual teachers in providing a range of suitable curriculum materials varies. It is highly unlikely that all student needs can be met by direct in-class support. This is the most visible and active of support mechanisms. It has constraints of time since it works best when the amount of in-class support is adequate enough to enable the programme of study to be sufficiently well known in advance so that the support can be geared precisely to the pupils' needs. The form in figure 3.3 has been used effectively to monitor this.

Time and timetable constraints frequently prevent extensive in-class support from reaching all the students who need help. Increasingly, this situation is leading to the special needs teachers acting in an advisory and monitoring capacity. One successful strategy is to develop support packs, the key elements of which can be pretaught and monitored in subsequent meetings. This is especially the case where key words need to be taught to enable a measure of independent learning to take place. It is also very useful to monitor programmes of work that are completed largely out of school, or at least out of that lesson. However, these strategies make at least two bland assumptions; the first that the pupils can read and the second that they will be sufficiently motivated to want to carry out extra work at times that keep them away from their friends. Neither of these assumptions can be relied upon. Where they do work best is when whoever is providing the linked support is seen by the students as caring about them as individuals. This provision of a personalised aspect of care brings about improvement in all areas of learning, not least in the difficult area of sustaining motivation. It is often easier to identify children who have a physical disability and to arrange specialist support for them because they can be placed on an external register. The difficulty is in ensuring that their needs are met in the normal classroom situation. This is part of the continuous awareness-raising that is part and parcel of implementing a whole-school policy.

Transmitting information about an individual

Extra support across the whole curriculum is rarely available even for the most needy pupils. An important part of special needs provision is in highlighting for staff concerns as they arise and in offering a support strategy. Figure 3.1 is a copy of a procedure form that allows areas of concern to be spread outwards among colleagues and allows feedback to come in to the special needs coordinator. It is extremely important that the individual does not get lost within the implementation of a whole-school policy. One of the strengths of the traditional remedial department was the caring atmosphere that was fostered. A key element in the whole-school approach is to make every child feel special. More and more it will be apparent that the way to bring about improvement is to show children that they are valued and to bring the provision of support into the light so that it is regarded no differently than a hearing aid or a pair of glasses. The ability to inspire children with confidence in themselves has a

NAME Mohammed	FORM 234I	D.O.B. 23/06/78	SUBJECT English									Attainment	
				RELEVANCE								NC AT	Level
SUBJECT NEEDS	STUDENT ABILITIES	STRATEGIES /ACTIVITIES		E	M	Sc	Tech	H	G	F			
1. Ability to read independently. 2. Ability to write at length. 3. Ability to follow oral instructions. 4. Ability to follow written instructions. 5. Ability to join in discussions in pairs and groups.	Finds board copying difficult. Cannot read competently at class reader level. Poor presentation. Does not form his letters correctly. Lacking in general punctuation skills. Generally weak at spelling. Finds it very difficult to produce a sustained piece of writing.	1. Mohammed has been placed on a structured reading scheme Fuzzbuzz. This is monitored outside of English as part of a supported self study activity. In class support is provided to develop confidence in listening to and following instructions. Mohammed issued with support folder containing: a) reading support materials 2. Class organisation involves multiple tasks allowing for differentiation by outcome. 3. Time for support has been made available after school		✓		✓		✓	✓			

Figure 3.3 Sheet used to monitor individual programmes of study

premium to be paid for in time. The special needs teacher is likely to be more and more a facilitator enabling children to function effectively in class and less and less purely a skilled practitioner in the basic skills. It is in this area as facilitator that careful consideration of procedures will pay large dividends, especially in time and record keeping.

Figure 3.4 shows the first stage of the concern procedure. In this illustration the intention quite deliberately is to focus on one small area. Although the advice seems quite banal, getting any group of teachers to agree to do anything consistently is very hard. A general policy on layout seems inappropriate once it gets down to specifics since different subject areas had different needs and views. It seems that a great deal of time could be spent discussing it and very little achieved. The result of this circulation of advice is that everyone can tackle and reinforce a specific area.

Figure 3.5 takes the use of the 'concern' sheet a stage further. The involvement of the parents is crucial to the success of a whole-school policy on special educational needs. Parental pressure to obtain the best education for their children may well be the best counterweight to financial restrictions but to be effective, parents need sound accurate information to make informed judgments. It is not enough to identify the problems. Having identified the problems or needs, parents are quite justified in asking, 'What are you as a school doing about it?'

The hardest aspect of any monitoring procedure is getting frequent feedback. In the example quoted, considerable information was passed on in an informal manner but, generally, staff were unwilling to commit it to paper. Investigation revealed that the most likely reason was that of subconscious prioritising whereby in the great paper chase only those items that were asked for again and again were completed. This situation is likely to improve as the value of the procedure is accepted.

One very positive outcome has been the response of the children involved. The fact that their problems can be shared, so that they are not either left to muddle along nor shamed by inappropriate demands, has led to a raising of their self-esteem. This is a vital part of the learning atmosphere. But again, having raised their expectations one cannot pull out of the support situation without leaving in place a change in the subject teaching that takes account of the needs of all pupils without just paying lip service to them.

A whole-school policy on special needs provision cannot operate in a vacuum. It presupposes, and may well be developed in tandem with, other policies which give a clear signal to pupils and parents that it is everyone's right to access the curriculum. The Education Reform Act 1988 has confirmed the position of schools as providers

NAME   Nigel M   DATE

FORM   F 1

CONCERN

In addition to other problems all areas of the curriculum have expressed concern that his poor presention seriously impairs communication and learning.

BACKGROUND

Nigel is left handed.
He has received Child Psychology Service support in the primary school. This help was mainly concentrated on improving his reading. He also has severe problems with his numeracy.

ACTION

subject teachers, it is recommended that there is a consistent approach to letter formation especially the letters 'b' ' e ' and ' a '. He should be encouraged to start these letters at the correct places.

It is recommended that he is encouraged to develop a larger script. Please note that there is a danger that attention to handwriting may cause some reversals in initial stages.

REVIEW

Figure 3.4 Sheet used to circulate information to staff

NAME _____   DATE _____

FORM   F 1 _____

CONCERN
Parental concern that Nigel is finding the work too hard. This is also linked to concern over bullying.

His parents have requested a meeting to discuss his needs and review his progress to date.

BACKGROUND
Nigel has a number of special educational needs including inadequate reading skills, poor spelling, generally weak language skills and severe problems with numeracy. He has received support from Child Psychology Service and is still under review. His extremely poor presentation tends to mask his progress.

ACTION
The Head of Lower School is following up the bullying.
Please return this sheet with any comments on progress or problems in the review section below.

REVIEW

Figure 3.5 Sheet used to circulate information to staff

of a service and the parents as its clients. In an attempt to increase or demonstrate schools' accountability to parents, it is now mandatory on schools to provide on request reasonably detailed programmes of study and clear procedures that allow parents to be able to see where their children stand in relation to the ATs and the POSs that their children are following. Children who have special educational needs are not exempt from these strictures even if they have a temporary exemption order. Support teaching presupposes that there is a programme of study to follow. The procedures illustrated in this chapter are one school's attempt to monitor effectively the needs of pupils who have special educational needs. Whilst the individual procedures in each school may vary, the need for procedures which allow progress to be plotted and recorded is overwhelming.

Part III
Teachers and support in action

4 Which support?: an examination of the term

Christopher Dyer

Changes in terminology

Fashions change: in education as in everything else. With changing fashion goes changing terminology. Educationally sub-normal children become pupils with learning difficulties. Of course, they remain the same children; the nature of their problems does not alter. The change in terms, however, might be said to reflect a different sensitivity on the part of the users. What has altered has been the climate of use. 'Sub-normal' is just a little too near to 'sub-human' for comfort. It would be encouraging to think that the change owed something to a thought process in education more profound than the tide of fashion. Alas, analysis of the nature of 'difficulty', how it is manifest and to what degree each of us gets 'into difficulties', often goes by default. The term is conveniently slotted into the gap left by the blue pencil line through earlier, now passé, terminology and Learning Difficulties (or LD) becomes the polite substitute for more derogatory labels, for any inconvenient pupil who cannot read, or do sums or write legibly. It even embraces the unkempt tearaways whose behaviour poses a threat to everyone's peace of mind — not least their own. The one recent attempt at legislative definition (in Section 1 (2) of the Education Act 1981) is tautologous in the extreme:

> a child has a *learning difficulty* if he has a significantly greater difficulty in learning than the majority of children of his age.

Perhaps as a positive response to potential confusion and certainly as an acknowledgement that learning difficulties are likely to be spread quite widely among a school population the fashion in dealing with the educational challenge they present has also shifted. Leaving aside the question of more dramatic disability (either physical or mental) which the Education Act 1981 also, conveniently, squeezes into the definition of learning difficulties (Section 1(2)(b)), schools are re-fashioning their approaches to the stream of pupils once called *remedial*. Wherever streaming itself is no longer rigidly practised (and that must be now the majority of schools) it has become logically impossible to segregate a number of pupils for an exclusively remedial treatment.

Primary schools have always, for the most part, followed what might be called a *whole-school approach*. Recently secondary schools have made this the banner under which questions of integrated teaching, mixed ability classes and curriculum studies can be best discussed (Luton 1986, Butt 1986). Along with this movement has come to the fore the term 'support' work (Fish 1986). The description is applied in such titles as Support Department, Support Teacher, Learning Support, Curriculum Support, and Special Needs Support. It is also a word used more colloquially in phrases such as, 'lack of support', 'support(ing) the idea', 'the support of my wife', 'I support integration', and many others. Herein lies its main difficulty. Any word that trips reasonably lightly off the tongue in common conversation is a grave risk when adopted as a quasitechnical term in specialist literature of any sort. One need look no further for another example than the procedures for implementing the Education Act 1981: it is no longer possible to make a statement about a child's problems without a confusion arising as to whether one is making a statement (7.(1)).

What do we mean by 'support'

The problem in seeking to annex the word *support* to be descriptive of an approach to meeting learning difficulties is its very diverse application generally. If I tell you that you are doing a great job, I may say that I am supporting you. On the other hand you, grateful for my words, may nevertheless feel that my deeds do not match them and complain that I am giving you no support whatsoever. Stung by the realisation, I might come into your classroom in my capacity as a support teacher only to find that what I thought of as support appeared to you to be intrusion.

Certainly this word should not be allowed to float about in education without some clear lines of common references. As Hart (1986) observes, 'The problem with trying to make any general evaluation of support teaching at this stage, however, is that no generally agreed definition of support teaching actually exists'. And she goes on to point out that the term also has educational currency in non-school based usages such as 'support teams' and 'support services'.

Nevertheless the term has crept into the currency of educational jargon. The 'support teacher' idea, at least as it is being applied to pupils with learning difficulties, may have had its first application to teachers providing help and guidance in classrooms where sensorially handicapped pupils were being maintained (Hegarty *et al.* 1981 p.124). It may have acquired currency, more generally as a description of the mutual support inherent in team teaching (Ferguson and Adams 1982). Whatever its antecedent, the term has now come to supplant the once current ethos of remedial education: not out of nothing has NARE recently changed the title of its journal from *Remedial Education* to *Support for Learning*. It should be noted, however, that in making the change the grammatical nature of the language used has changed. *Remedial* education implies almost a status: a distinct type of education with the possibility of its own rules of judgement and even curriculum. *Support for Learning*, in supplanting it, shifts the syntax into the active mode and implies interventionist strategies at the point of delivery where teaching and learning meet. This shift of emphasis reflects the current debate within schools about developing a broad and appropriate curriculum: at the same time, examining the way it is presented to pupils. It is essentially a recognition of the right of pupils to a common education even if some find the going tough. But in that case whom is the support teacher supporting: the deliverer or the recipient? Who needs the underpinning? If the support is 'for learning', which aspects of the learning?

And what about the growing number of support departments in schools? If they are not to be remedial departments under another name, in other words if their image is to differ, in what way are they going to assert their function?

All these questions, along with others that will inevitably arise as debate continues, can only be answered if the term *support* itself is clearly defined. It is, after all, acquiring to itself a technical usage. To prevent confusion and to ensure that current educational trends do not end up as non-educational confusion, it must be prevented from becoming a humpty-dumpty word meaning whatever anyone chooses to make it mean, independent of anyone else. As schools experiment with different ways of organising access to the curriculum for low achievers (McCall 1980) so each will be tempted to label its version 'support'.

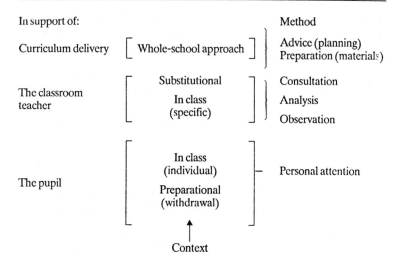

Figure 4.1   Three strands of emphasis in considering which support is desirable

The purpose of support

Perhaps the following qualifications of the term could be used to help clarify what is going on and allow for a clearer and more exact usage. There appear to be three main applications for which support may be offered:

1. to an individual pupil, or small group of pupils directly;
2. to teacher colleagues who have pupils with learning difficulties in their class or group;
3. in order to facilitate the delivery of the curriculum by influencing directly the choice, presentation or administration of teaching materials.

The nature of the support

Within these broad categories, further more detailed applications can be defined.

1 Direct pupil support (or one-to-one support)

This is given when an experienced teacher deals with individual difficulties directly with the pupil concerned either:

(a) *In-class support* where the teacher is available, as the pupil works in-class to obviate problems for the pupil (or group of pupils) as they arise in the lesson:

(b) *Preparational support* where the teacher, on an individual basis, seeks to get ahead of the problem by preparing a pupil for coming lessons: e.g. by seeking to teach sight vocabulary of key words upon which the next lessons will hinge. This implies that the teacher will already have had discussions with a subject or class teacher involving lesson plans for some time ahead.

(c) *Remedial support* The two sub-divisions already described would seem to be the limit of individual attention to pupils that fits in with the usage of *support* as it appears in recent literature (Visser 1986). There are schools, however, where previous models of provision for low achievers are more or less adhered to and where pupils are withdrawn into a separate group or class. This may be for most of the teaching time or be timetabled more specifically (e.g. to miss one subject in order to have extra tuition in reading or number work). Some of this provision is now called *support* but may have very little impact on the whole-school approach. In most schools, however, some moves towards a level of integrated working are taking place. To indicate such a state and the possibility of its being transitional it might be best to combine both 'old' and 'new' terminology and call the provision remedial support.

2 Teacher/pupil support

In some practices the distinction between being of direct assistance to the teacher and to the pupils is necessarily blurred. One example would be:

(a) *General class support* — this is really a method of enhancing the pupil/teacher ratio of certain classes where there are a number of pupils with difficulties, without necessarily singling them out. In essence it is a team-teaching situation and, ideally, does not distinguish roles between the teachers concerned. It is a method of dealing with problems that may not necessarily involve teachers specifically appointed to SEN posts. Where that is the case, then the teachers concerned might, in turn, look for other forms of *support* (see below). This is a caution, therefore, not to take any of the distinctions made in this article as being exclusive. In any given situation several functions of support, which can be identified separately, may be happening simultaneously.

(b) *Consultative support* — picks up this very point. Where there is no direct involvement of specialist SEN staff, their support on a consultative basis is of considerable value. Essentially the nature of *consultation* is to respond to the problems of the moment but the role is to be available to colleagues to discuss, to plan and to 'get ahead' of potential problems that lessons might present for pupils with learning difficulties. Where ancillary help is provided for the everyday needs of a pupil, access to this consultation is particularly important. It is often within the consultative framework that schools receive or draw on help from outside their own resources, for example from special schools that are now, increasingly, providing outreach services within their own specialities.

(c) *Analytical support* may be seen as one response to a specific problem that is identified during *consultation*. What the class teacher will be seeking to tap, in this instance, is the experience of an SEN support teacher to detect what might be going wrong either in the organisation and preparation of lesson materials or in the learning style of a particular pupil. The role of the 'analyst' calls for some tact on the part of any support teacher, especially where it becomes obvious that a fault lies in the teaching rather than in the learning! Solutions to problem areas identified under analysis might develop from other specific support options, such as . . .

(d) *Observational support* where the support teacher comes into a lesson with the intention of observing a specific point either of a pupil's learning strategy or of classroom organisation and lesson presentation. It is usually desirable to follow up 'hunches' that develop when listening to accounts of difficulties during consultation or analysis by direct observation. Sometimes, it is the more profitable to allow the class teacher to have the chance to undertake the observation since he or she is the person who will have to implement any 'solution'. In this case the role of the SEN teacher might be . . .

(e) *Substitutional support* In some circumstances it is good practice for the support teacher to take over teaching a lesson. There has to be more than a little mutual confidence among staff (mutual support, in fact) for this mode of working to slip easily into schedules. To a large extent, in subject-based teaching loads, it depends on the level of competence and confidence which the support teacher may have in the area concerned. It can also be ineffective if it is too unusual a circumstance so that teachers and pupils carry out the exercise in a spirit of mutual embarrassment and no observation of what normally happens can then take place. It often works best as a strategy in primary schools with the luxury of some support provision. For example: the deputy head of an infant school, as part of a one-term secondment course, chose to organise her 'in-school' assignment work, to allow teachers to make observations of pupils while she taught the classes. What was then written up were the insights the teachers had gained, rather than the individual gain of the deputy head and the whole report was set in the context of what emerged as a whole-school policy. As a function it may also be used within the team teaching situation outlined at 2 (a) above.

(f) *Specific (in-class) support* may also be a follow-up to analysis of a difficulty. Where a flaw is identified in a specific learning strategy in a pupil, it may be profitable to seek to remediate it on-task alongside the pupil. The drawback is that it might serve to emphasise the pupil's problem and draw unnecessary attention to the individual. It is probably to be recommended only as a specific focus where direct pupil in-class support (1 (a) above) is already practised; otherwise . . .

(g) *Specific withdrawal support* may be preferable for a short span of time, as part of the general support strategy. This is often the model used by peripatetic teachers of the visually or the hearing impaired, for specific testing or guidance.

3 Support in curriculum delivery

While all the above options are concerned directly with teaching, which itself is curriculum delivery, there are also functions that SEN teachers may undertake at one stage back from the classroom floor.

(a) *Planning support* may be seen as a particular function of 2 (b) and (c) when lesson plans are being drawn up: to identify potential pitfalls for pupils (or for a specific pupil) in the content and presentation of a syllabus. For instance, it is often the language of the classroom, both spoken and written, that gets in the way of the pupil with learning difficulties. It is not always easy or desirable for a subject teacher to be in a state of constant self-criticism when setting out the subject. It can be helpful, however, to allow the SEN teacher to look at the presentation through the eyes of a pupil in difficulties and suggest where extra steps need to be inserted, to elucidate metaphorical language or explain special usages of words with common meanings, and so on. Equally important the SEN teacher might suggest that less information is presented and concentrate on the absolute minimum that would make simple clear sense to the pupil without losing what the subject teacher considered essential. This may well involve . . .

(b) *Material (preparation) support* This, too, ought to follow careful analysis of the needs within any given situation. The need, for example, is generally not to prepare endless 'simplified' worksheets, although sometimes this is desirable, but to identify and help to establish ways in which commonly used materials might be made accessible to certain pupils. For example it might be that, rather than rewrite pages of a rather dry textbook, the essential knowledge it contains could be lifted from the paper by a pupil in difficulty through the simple device of highlighting *key* words. The preparation role, in this instance, would be to identify these key words which carry the idea and then establish their recognition (perhaps via 2(g) above) rather than labour over rewriting the whole text. Again, the preparation of an 'individual tape' for a pupil, especially in these days of seemingly universal possession of Walkman facilities, might both be stimulating to a pupil with reading problems and service to access a lesson far better than poorly reproduced worksheets. There is plenty of opportunity for imaginative support in finding ways around difficulties.

(c) *Curriculum support* It is not easy to be definitive over a topic as wide as 'the curriculum'. Everyone thinks they know what a curriculum is; yet it remains hard to define. Any SEN support teacher, now or in the future, cannot avoid being drawn into the debates about what curriculum is to be delivered and how the delivery is to be evaluated. All that has gone before in this paper has been about curriculum matters in one form or another. Throughout, however, there has been one so far unvoiced assumption; that the purpose of any support is to key pupils in, as far as possible, to the general curriculum available to all. There may, of course, be different emphases for many different pupils in the options available in secondary schools. There must not, however, be a separate curriculum with prescribed and lesser options to which pupils with learning difficulties are gravitated. In a sense the 'curriculum support' necessary, from support teachers especially, is support for the integrity of the curriculum itself.

HMI (1986) noted that, in regard to low attainers, '. . . for some schools curriculum development has been piecemeal, lacking effective coordination across the curriculum for these pupils. (148) . . . If attainment is to be raised, many schools need to give more rigorous thought to what their lower attaining pupils can and should attain (149)'. In giving thought not only to the content of the curriculum but also to facilitating learning strategies, social participation and general personality and development for SEN pupils, support teachers may take a lead in improving educational attainment generally for all pupils. After all, just because many pupils do manage to learn from some textbooks demanding a reading age of 14+, does it mean that that is the most effective way for them to learn? Might not alternative strategies, thought out on behalf of pupils who find it difficult, be turned to good effect by all pupils?

Conclusion

The support department

This article has sought to set out some, hopefully most, of the possible ways of offering *support* within a school that might be implicit in a casual use of 'I'm a support teacher' or 'we operate a support policy in this school'. In doing this, it is not the intention to suggest that all schools must operate all forms of support nor that one is necessarily better than another. The appropriateness or otherwise of the support given can only be determined by taking account of the particular factors operating for one pupil (or group of pupils) in one school situation at the time. Categorising the possible support, however, should enable discussion to take place with some precision on the nature of the need and the means available to meet it. The question posed in the title, 'Which support?' is really only half a question. The full text, supplied by each school would be, 'Which support is desirable at this point in our school's development?' 'Which support is economically possible' — and so on. Inevitably, the emphasis in this article has tended to slip towards secondary working since the arguments have sprung out of changes in remedial department approaches over recent years. Enough hints have been dropped along the way, however, for it to be seen that the principle of support working, in one or another particular application, can apply to primary practice. Indeed, primary practice has been ahead of the field in many ways to the extent of providing an accepted model for some secondary schools who are looking to re-jig their organisation and curriculum throughout the transitional year between junior and secondary schools at 11+ − 12+. (The 'first year' which often poses the most problems to pupils with degrees of learning difficulty transferring into both a larger school and into teaching demanding different learning strategies.)

With the change of emphasis in secondary schools, however, comes the redesignation of that part of the operation that used to care for 'the remedial group'. In the new nomenclature, it will probably have support as part of its title − perhaps: the Support Department. If it is to function effectively it will need to define how its operation is to be presented and what it can deliver. One thing that the previous remedial streams often did very effectively, whatever else they did questionably, was to succeed in giving some personal status and self-respect to their (withdrawn) pupils. The newer departments may well establish a role that encompasses some aspects of the working models outlined above. There is, however, still the need for them to continue the good traditions of the past; when dealing with pupils with learning difficulties, to support their own self-respect.

Acknowledgement

I gratefully acknowledge the help of advisor colleagues from neighbouring boroughs in the preparation of this article: T Bailey, B Canvin, R Gerken, P Townley and B Whitelaw.

References

Butt, N. (1986) Implementing the whole school approach at secondary level. *Support for Learning*, **1**, 4 pp 11-21.
DES (1986) *A survey of the lower attaining pupils' programme: the first two years.* HMSO.
Ferguson, N. and Adams, M. (1982) Assessing the advantages of team teaching in remedial education: the remedial teacher's role *Remedial Education*, **17**, 1.
Fish, J. (1986) (Chair) *Educational opportunities for all?* Report to the Inner London Education Authority.
Hart, S. (1986) Evaluating support teaching *Gnosis*, **9**, pp 26-31.
Hegarty S., Pocklington, K. and Lucas, D. (1981) *Educating pupils with special needs in ordinary school*, Windsor: NFER-Nelson.
Luton, K. (1986) Learning by doing: the development of a whole school approach. *Support for Learning*, **1**, 4 pp 22-31.
McCall. C. (1980) Ways of providing for low achievers in the secondary school: suggested advantages, disadvantages and alternatives. *Educational Review*, Occasional Publications, University of Birmingham.
Visser, J. (1986) Support: a description of the work of the SEN professional. *Support for Learning*, **1**, 4 pp 5-9.

5 Accessing the curriculum for children with special educational needs: towards a meta-model

Charles W. Gains

Provision for children with learning difficulties has excited the imagination of educationalists for many decades. The challenge of opening up the world of learning to bewildered and struggling pupils has produced a vast range of detailed strategies and techniques. Indeed, it is fair to say that no area of education has attracted so much debate, research and experimentation. This, inevitably, has produced its share of prophets, disciples and protagonists of every conceivable hue. They have bombarded us with opinion and advice, and vigorously canvassed support. The fact that much of this is highly suspect, even contradictory, has led to a lot of confusion in the ranks of those invested with the responsibility of educating such pupils. The general effect is that while some have received highly specific and possibly useful help, the majority have drifted along in a world of half-baked theory and traditional 'hand-me-down' techniques and ideas. Sadly, this has meant many pupils are simply kept occupied and entertained, not properly educated.

This is not to deny the considerable progress that has undoubtedly been made but this remains isolated and fragmented. Clearly it is a nonsense that there is such a wide disparity in provision and one must challenge the regular teacher statement that '. . . it works for me'. Basic learning difficulties are amazingly universal. For example, I have witnessed in Northern India pupils using an entirely different alphabet but transposing and reversing letters in exactly the same manner as our own children with severe learning difficulties. Given such evidence, it should be possible for professionals everywhere to arrive at some common philosophy, set of guiding principles and some general agreement on appropriate strategies and techniques. This chapter attempts to move the reader in that direction.

The historical drift

Some provision for pupils with learning difficulties has always been made, even if this was only to 'stream' them crudely. But in the years following World War II determined efforts were made to get more specific help to troubled pupils on a systematic basis. This led to the growth of 'remedial education' and remedial teachers both within schools and on peripatetic teams. The principal means used to identify pupils in need of help was the standardised tests and gaps between potential and performance were eagerly sought. Programmes were developed in the basic subject areas that purported to accelerate learning. These 'retarded' pupils would be spirited away from their colleagues, often during a most interesting lesson, and bustled off to some remote corner of a school for 'treatment'. Thus arose the 'medical model', something we have never quite managed to dispel. In spite of all this, examples of good practice flourished and were developed to sophisticated levels.

The evidence for the effectiveness of this approach was, at best, ambiguous. Collins (1961), for example, produced a most devastating denunciation of withdrawal methods. His research suggested that while it was relatively easy to produce short-term remedial gains in reading these were 'washed out' in the longer term. Oddly enough this claim was made nearly a decade later for the supposed ineffectiveness of the American-inspired compensatory programmes. On reflection, it is incredible that no major investigation into the effectiveness of remedial intervention has ever taken place in spite of a massive expansion of services from the mid-1960s onwards. This was yet another demonstration in education of faith triumphing over evidence. Still, and for some unfathomable reason, the work regularly attracted gifted practitioners who made major impacts on thinking. It was, of course, a time of hope and optimism reaching its zenith with the publication of the Warnock Report in 1978. The bits of Warnock that filtered through into the 1981 Education Act encouraged practitioners into thinking that a new dawn had arrived. The integration of pupils with special needs into mainstream activity was accepted in theory if not always in practice. There was much talk of 'in-class support' and 'whole-school' approaches but expectations were not to be fully met. Even before the 1988 Education Reform Act came into being, local authorities were under increasing financial pressure, a situation that has worsened even more rapidly since. The effect has been a gradual erosion of traditional provision within schools and with little to take its place. There is no doubt that increasing numbers of pupils are potentially at risk.

However, all is not gloom. The introduction of the National Curriculum enshrines in law the rights of all pupils, with very few exceptions, to the same curriculum. No longer can many pupils be conveniently marginalised. The entitlement to a whole curriculum poses huge problems for the profession but equally a tremendous challenge. It constitutes, in effect, the first opportunity in about 40 years, to invent the game from scratch. If special educators are to respond to this challenge a number of fundamental questions need to be addressed:

1. How should we now re-define special educational needs?
2. What effect will this have on teaching roles?
3. What new organisational adjustments will need to be made?
4. Will we need to extend our range of teaching models?
5. What materials and resources will be needed to implement the above?

Re-defining special educational needs

In this field definitions abound. The lack of clarity has often bedevilled attempts to reach those with learning problems. The National Association for Remedial Education (NARE) faced this tricky issue some years ago and came up with the following:

> Remedial education is that part of education which is concerned with the prevention, investigation and treatment of learning difficulties from whatsoever source they may emanate and which hinder the normal educational development of the student.
> (NARE Guidelines No 1 *Report on In-service Training*, 1977)

The above was deliberately intended to be as broad as possible, and to encompass the whole range of difficulties caused by cognitive, social, emotional or physical factors. In the light of developments we now need to move on a little. The following is offered for consideration:

> Special educational needs refer to the needs of students which constrain them from having full access to the curriculum and extra-curricular activities of a school or institution that are enjoyed by their contemporaries. There is a considerable range of handicap which might prevent this, namely physical, social, emotional, intellectual or simply poor prior educational experience. The nature of the difficulty encountered may be temporary or mild, intermediate or moderate, long-term or severe. Thus defined, it is impossible to identify needs by simple measures and it is conceivable that almost all students will, at some point, experience a learning difficulty which impedes normal progress. The purpose of this definition is to avoid the labels, categories and deficit models that have, in the past, led to over-simplistic responses and treatment. Thus conceived, special educational needs are not peripheral to mainstream activity but part of the general curriculum delivery to all students.

Clearly the above would need wider discussion and refinement but until the profession has some agreed definition of what constitutes special educational needs we cannot effectively harness the resources to deal with it.

Titles and roles

Those on the receiving end of special provision have been variously known as 'backward', 'slow learners', 'low attainers', 'under-achievers' and so on. Christopher Dyer (1991) has traced this development and the cul-de-sac it has led us into. Similarly, we have had 'special education', 'remedial education', 'compensatory education' and currently 'support work'. To add to this, we are invited to think of difficulties as 'mild', 'moderate' and 'severe'. All this does to the lay person is convey the notion of acute indecision. It also, sadly, indicates that there are groups of students who are 'special' and who should somehow be dealt with separately. My own preference would be to shift the discussion to 'underachievement' which might take in a massive 40 per cent of all pupils and bring to decision-makers the fact that learning difficulty is common and widespread. In view of current debates on standards of literacy and numeracy this would be a singularly opportune moment to make such a case.

All this confuses teacher roles and the author has collected over 20 different descriptions ranging from 'remedial teacher' to the currently popular 'special needs coordinator'. Again NARE, in an attempt to clarify the situation, has issued a guideline on roles (NARE 1985). Here the 'model' special needs coordinator is seen as fulfilling the following:

— an assessment role;
— a prescriptive role;
— a teaching/pastoral role;
— a supportive role;
— a liaison role;
— a management role;
— a staff development role.

Events have moved on with such rapidity that even this would now need reworking. For example, Alan Dyson profers a radical view of how the role needs to adapt to the demands of the current decade (Dyson 1990, 1991). Similarly the National Council for Special Education has produced an informative booklet on how the content of teachers' courses should be modified (NCSE 1990). Slowly, and at times a little painfully, we appear to be moving towards some consensus of what roles and skills the professional of the future will require.

Organisational structures

The National Curriculum has shifted the focus away from content and towards delivery. This, plus the effects of finance-led decision-making, indicates an urgent need for a re-examination of organisational structures. As currently organised, special needs provision is both expensive and of limited effect. In the past, the nature of school management was to accept the inevitable cost and to marginalise special needs. This option is increasingly less available to management. Where then might we look for systems that will enable us to maximise delivery and simultaneously be cost-effective?

One thinks immediately of general systems theory, for example Miller (1978). Briefly systems theory can enable us to see relationships between variables and how theories and strategies can best be put together to solve problems. Systems theory suggests that:

1. The child must be viewed as the product of a system of units that interact.
2. Behaviour is the product of multiple causes rather than unitary causes.
3. If you tamper with one part of the system without regard to the total system, it can have a negative effect.

4. Complex processes demand multi-level and inter-disciplinary approaches.
5. Planned intervention at several points can produce a powerful synergistic, or 'ripple' effect.
6. Curriculum development and analysis of learning styles go hand-in-hand.

An excellent example of the above can be found in Ramey *et al.* (1982). They successfully apply the general systems model to explain the possible prevention of developmental retardation. The application of this model is yet to find general acceptance here although it is increasingly creeping into the diagnosis and treatment of behavioural difficulties, for example Cooper and Upton (1991). Similarly, we are slow to take advantage of planning theory (Faludi 1988) and of systems thinking pioneered by people such as Peter Checkland (1981).

Generally we have got ourselves bogged down in structures and systems from the past that were more concerned with keeping pupils away from mainstream curriculum than with integrating them. Now that option is drying up, we need to take a much more serious look at management structures, to acknowledge the multiplicity of variables that contribute to learning failure and, through the adaptation of the logistics of school delivery, devise a more potent system of dealing with special educational needs. We are barely at the beginning of this fascinating development.

Classroom teaching models

The most favoured teaching model used in dealing with learning problems is that of mastery learning theory. It is also the most misunderstood and abused. The basic features will be familiar to the reader:

— Mastery is defined in terms of stating the particular objectives each pupil should achieve.
— The instruction should be broken down into well-defined units.
— Each unit should be mastered before proceeding to the next unit.
— Formative tests are to be administered at the completion of each unit to provide feedback information.
— Original instruction is to be supplemented with correctives if necessary.
— The timing is to be varied to suit the pupil.

Mastery learning is undoubtedly a powerful tool in a teacher's armoury. Unfortunately it has been largely hijacked by certain behaviourists, particularly in the form of precision teaching, and reduced to a boring 'tick and response' routine. It has far greater application than that. The author has experimented with its use in a more flexible way in the field of early childhood education (Gains and Pritlove 1985). To understand fully and appreciate the usefulness of mastery approaches, one must return to some of the original sources such as Block (1971) and Bloom (1976) and also to more recent research such as that of Arlin (1984) and Guskey and Gates (1986).

Mastery is indeed a powerful tool but is by no means the only model that can be deployed. An overview of teaching models is available in the seminal work of Bruce Joyce and Marsha Weil (1986). Joyce and Weil classify teaching models under four headings: the information processing family; the personal family; the social family; and the behavioural systems family. Within this framework there are individual models many of which have implications for dealing with learning failure. It is staggering that most practitioners have only the vaguest idea of two or three. The author has taken the liberty of laying out the models identified by Joyce and Weil with some minor amendments (figure 5.1). One model, that of mastery learning because of its previously stated importance, is moved to one side. In addition, thinking skills and construct theory have been introduced. The importance of teaching thinking skills has been stressed on many occasions by both Edward deBono and Reuven Feuerstein. The work of Matthew Lipman is less well appreciated although a recent article has brought it to the notice of special needs coordinators (Robinson 1991). Similarly Kelly's construct theory, while known to many, is only just beginning to surface as a useful strategy (Ashley 1991).

The purpose of the above is not to overwhelm readers but to remind them of the rich array of alternatives available. For a long time we have got by with a mishmash of techniques loosely based, at best, on recognisable models. If we are to sharpen our delivery we have to take advantage of the best tools we can find, not simply re-work some tired old methods.

Materials and resources

Earlier simplistic notions of what constitutes appropriate materials for poor learners is under scrutiny now there is a National Curriculum requirement to deliver a range of subjects. The previous focus on basic skills meant specialist teachers had only to gather

Information Processing	Personal	Social	Behaviour Modification
Help us to understand . . . how to handle information how to organise data how to solve problems how to generate concepts how we employ verbal and non-verbal symbols	Help us to understand . . . feelings and emotions the uniqueness of the individual the long term development of individual the need for pastoral support affective education	Help us to understand . . . social relations how individuals interact with each other the democratic process	Help us to understand . . . how human behaviour is shaped and formed how activities are sequenced
Use . . . specific teaching approaches methods, materials	Use . . . interviews, discussions, self discovery, creative writing	Use . . . group investigations co-operation in tasks	Use . . . systematic programmes rewards
Attaining concepts (J Bruner)	Non-directive (C Rogers)	Group investigation (J Dewey)	Self control (BF Skinner)
Thinking inductively (H Taba)	Synectics (W Gordon)	Role playing (F & G Shaftel)	Direct instruction (BF Skinner)
Inquiry Training (R Suchman)	Awareness Training (W Schutz)	Jurisprudential (D Oliver & J Shaver)	Simulations (Various)
Advance Organisers (D Ausubell)	Classroom meeting (W Glasser)	Laboratory Training (NTL)	Assertive training (J Wolpe)
Memorisation (H Lorayne and J Lucas)		Social science inquiry (B Massialas and B Cox)	
Developing intellect (J Piaget)			
Biological science (J Schwab)			
Mastery Learning (B Bloom)			
Thinking skills (E DeBono, R Feuerstein, M Lipman)			
Construct theory (GA Kelly)			

Figure 5.1   Models of teaching (Adapted from Joyce and Weil (1986)

together a range of books and games, supplemented with home-made materials. Undoubtedly, a lot of skill and ingenuity went into this task to the benefit of pupils. Now we need to move on and translate this expertise into the demands of the contemporary situation. There is a need for a complete overhaul of materials and techniques. In particular, we have to develop sophisticated means of 'bridging the gap' to the National curriculum. This, hopefully, will take us several steps beyond the traditional worksheet. One must also take cognizance of the technology which appears daily to arrive on our doorstep, the potential of which is yet to be fully grasped. It's time once more to turn our imaginations loose.

Summary

This chapter has set out to identify those elements of a possible meta-model for meeting the curricular needs of pupils with learning difficulty. It is the belief of the author that we now have the knowledge and the means to make massive inroads into a problem we have struggled with for decades. It still is like having the ingredients of an interesting recipe without much idea of the finished product. However, we seem to be edging towards a 'master plan' of some sort that will both clarify our thinking and direct our energies.

References

Arlin, M. (1984) 'Time, equality and mastery learning' *Review of Educational Research* **54**, 1.
Ashley, J. (1991) 'Personal constructs — an alternative approach?' *Support for Learning*, **6**, 2.
Block, J.H. (ed.) (1971) *Mastery Learning: Theory and Practice*, London: Holt, Rinehart and Winston.
Bloom, B.S. (1976) *Human Characteristics and School Learning*, London: *McGraw Hill*.
Checkland, P. (1981) *Systems Thinking, Systems Practice*, London: John Wiley.
Collins, J.E. (1961) *The Effects of Remedial Education*, University of Birmingham.
Cooper, P. and Upton, G. (1991) 'Controlling the urge to control: An ecosystemic approach to problem behaviour in schools' *Support for Learning*, **6**, 1.
DES (1978) *Special Educational Needs* (The Warnock Report), London: HMSO.
Dyer, C. (1991) 'An end to the slow lane: A critique of the term 'slow learner' and its lingering usage' *Support for Learning*, **6**, 2.
Dyson, A. (1990) 'Effective learning consultancy: A future role for special needs coordinators?' *Support for Learning*, **5**, 3.
Dyson, A. (1991) 'Rethinking roles, rethinking concepts: Special needs teachers in mainstream schools' *Support for Learning*, **6**, 2.
Faludi, A. (ed.) (1988) *A Reader in Planning Theory*, Oxford: Pergamon.
Gains, C.W. and Pritlove, S.A. (1985) *The Humberside Early Learning Project*, Humberside County Council.

Guskey, T.R. and Gates, S.L. (1986) 'Synthesis of research on the effects of mastery learning in elementary and secondary classrooms' *Educational Leadership*, May.

Joyce, B. and Weil, M. (1986) *Models of Teaching*, New York: Prentice Hall.

Miller, J.G. (1978) *Living Systems*, London: McGraw Hill.

NARE (1977) Guidelines No 1 *Report on In-service Training*, National Association for Remedial Education.

NARE (1985) Guidelines No 6 *Teaching Roles for Special Educational Needs*, National Association for Remedial Education.

NCSE (1990) *Guidelines to the Content of Teachers' Courses in Special Educational Needs*, National Council for Special Education.

Ramey, C.T., MacPhee, D. and Yeates, K.O. (1982) 'Preventing developmental retardation: A general systems model' in Bond, L. and Joffe, J. (eds) *Facilitating Infant and Early Childhood Development*, University of New England Press.

Robinson, W. (1991) 'Rich seams of mind' *Support for Learning*, **6**, 3.

6 Curriculum access for all

Tricia Barthorpe

With the introduction of the National Curriculum in 1989 there appeared a jargonistic disease only identifiable as the 'BBRDs'. Rearing its head in the majority of National Curriculum publications and on most staff development courses requiring National Curriculum funding, the disease originally emanated from the city of York. Supposedly, being first discovered by Dr. N.C.C., its medical name was derived from the initials of four of the most frequently misused and misunderstood words in curriculum technology, Broad, Balanced, Relevant and Differentiated. Unfortunately, although much has been written, as yet little can be identified and translated into recovery in the classroom. The only research at present being undertaken is by very conscientious, hard-working practitioners in 'on the job' training. Suitable definitions, precise meanings and translations of theory into practice, are a rare commodity and this will prove difficult to remedy until the educational world has recovered from the onslaught and inundation of recent legislation and non-statutory guidance. However, in order to assist future sufferers and enable curriculum access for all, which was the ultimate aim of Curriculum Guidance 2, *A Curriculum for All*, (NCC 1989) the following thoughts may assist with curriculum planning.

Broad

First indications of how broad the National Curriculum was to be, were hinted at by the priority given to the ten basic subjects of the curriculum, plus RE. Further priority was then given to the three core subjects of English, Mathematics and Science. The vast majority of practitioners will agree that all pupils are entitled to a broad curriculum. However, should breadth in the curriculum only be identifiable by the subjects on offer? Thought should also be given to the breadth of attainment targets being offered. For those pupils with special educational needs, will there now be too broad a curriculum available, rather than a necessary and relevant in-depth curriculum? Will we swing too far away from the very narrow curriculum previously on offer to a situation where pupils sample a little of everything and become masters of nothing? The curricular entitlement for all pupils must be preserved at all costs, but the breadth of the curriculum should be tailored to the individual needs and requirements of those pupils concerned. Possible side-effects of this very broad ten subject curriculum may be the loss of what became recognised by Hargreaves (1982) as the 'hidden curriculum'. The value of this element of the curriculum should never be under-estimated as invariably it has led to the image and ethos of a school and thus the school's own reputation. The breadth of education available to all participants in the school will invariably need to be a very rigorous and conscientious balancing act carried out by able management.

Balance

Thoughts of balance in the curriculum have tended to lead practitioners into the subject areas again and towards the allocation of time. In the past, proportional amounts of time, resources and teacher-hours have been awarded to those areas deemed to have the highest priority. Many schools discovered untold dilemmas when faced with curriculum returns because they had to identify curriculum areas taught in percentage terms. Under ERA (1988) high allocations of time and resource will, in future, have to be given to both the core and foundation subjects. Hopefully, this will not lead to the omission, or second-class status, of other subjects such as home economics, where very many pupils with special educational needs found success. Still, the most difficult balancing act for teachers will be in the allocation of time necessary for pupils to complete the task being asked and the weighing up of what has to be omitted from the curriculum in order to provide it. Choices will have to be made between the attainment targets offered and those desperately needed by the pupil. Awareness of the balance needed in time, interest and pace in a classroom and creating opportunities for those to happen, are the hall-marks of a good learning environment. The provision of 'hoop jumping' in order to satisfy other 'criteria', for example Checklists and SATs can be a dangerous path for a pupil with learning problems. Good practice comes from knowing the balancing act that teachers perform daily when the workload for pupils is stimulating, challenging and relevant to their individual needs.

Relevant

As outlined in *Curriculum Access for All* (NARE 1990) a relevant curriculum should be active and experiential, also taking into account the differences in pupils' interests, methods and materials. Opportunities should be provided to enable pupils to participate in a wide range of experiences relevant to their needs. Like all pupils, those with special educational needs, make the maximum possible progress when tasks undertaken take into account their particular strengths and weaknesses, their first-hand experiences and their needs, in an age-related context. By working in a differentiated learning situation a pupil comes to recognise, establish, generalise and transfer information into other situations as he/she deems necessary. However, for the child experiencing learning difficulties the pace at which relevant, active learning takes place will be a very important factor. Moreover the learning environment has to be established so that the most relevant of work can actually commence. Relevant tasks will not always secure good behaviour for the teacher, on the other hand irrelevant tasks are often the root cause of poor behaviour. Thus, in assisting the relevance of work to all pupils in the class, differentiation of work will need to be carefully thought through and planned by the class teacher.

Differentiated

Pupil's entitlement to the National Curriculum should be one of a broad, balanced and differentiated curriculum relevant to their needs, differentiation being based on an understanding of individual differences and the worth and value of each pupil's learning. Warnock (1978) stated:

> The purpose of education for all children is the same; the goals are the same. But the help that individual children need in progressing towards them will be different.

As outlined in *Differentiation: Your Responsibility* (Barthorpe and Visser 1991) differentiation is based on an understanding of individual differences. In order to differentiate, teachers will need:

— a clear understanding of the ways in which children learn;
— an analysis of the knowledge and skills which comprise a particular learning task;
— a heightened awareness of possible obstacles to successful learning, some of which might unwittingly be caused by teachers themselves;
— procedures for observing children on task in the learning situation;
— an understanding of the ways in which this data can be utilised in order to structure learning situations which will ensure success for pupils with special needs;
— to work closely with colleagues who have specialised knowledge and expertise in the area of special needs;
— knowledge of designing and implementing carefully structured programmes which enable learning to take place in successful steps.

Mention should also be made of the different teaching styles for differentiation and differing pupils' learning styles. Thus classroom organisation plays a critical role in planning for differentiation. An example of this kind of working can be the jigsaw model for example, where the class is split into groups of equal size. All members of the 'home group' are identified with a different task necessary for the completion of the work such as publicity/costing/ production/quality control. Regular meetings take place between all the expert 'publishers' or 'producers' from all the groups but each must report back to their home group and provide their own piece of expertise in order for the task to be completed. Provided tasks set are achievable, all pupils play a very significant role in the overall production of the finished article.

Access to curriculum

Thus the BBRDs have entered into educational jargon and will remain until their flavour diminishes at the end of the month. We need to ask when and how does an understanding of the terminology assist the teacher in ensuring curriculum access for all? Perhaps a first stage could be the curriculum development plan for the school. Curriculum planning between the whole teaching staff and others involved in its delivery plays a very important role in enabling access. The curriculum development plan as an integral part of the school management plan should be devised through the use of four processes:

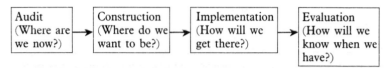

| Audit (Where are we now?) | → | Construction (Where do we want to be?) | → | Implementation (How will we get there?) | → | Evaluation (How will we know when we have?) |

The plan should *review* existing curriculum practice. The availability and allocation of resources, staffing and future implications for staff development all play a critical part. The plan should *revise* existing curricular practice and schemes of work securing that the broad aims of the overall curriculum are being met. Thought must be given to present provision in books, materials, IT and the whole-school policies in other areas will need checking in order to ascertain the ways in which they impinge on the curriculum plan.

Finally, the mode of reporting on the curriculum to parents, governors and others will need full discussion. Thought should also be given to the establishment of monitoring and evaluation procedures. Too often in curriculum planning the evaluation exercise appears at the end of the exercise without any prior thought as to what was originally being established. Often a lack of stated criteria makes it impossible for the curriculum to be evaluated objectively. Suitable criteria may be the audit, construction, implementation and evaluation model and should be phrased in such a manner that what is being tackled can be measured objectively. Behaviourist terminology can often be quite helpful here. As the curriculum plan evolves and changes during the year it becomes more and more difficult to establish what the original criteria were, the reasoning behind the changes made and why the final version was arrived upon. The plan should also *ensure* that all the staff involved in it know of the curriculum policy for those pupils who have special educational needs and that they are aware of the numerous methods available for giving them access to the curriculum. A designated member of staff responsible for coordinating the whole-school policy on special educational needs and also for informing all staff how to provide access to the curriculum for all pupils is a vital member of the curriculum management team.

In the formation of the curriculum development plan, the schemes of work will form its core.

Aims and objectives

The aims and objectives of the curriculum should be fully set out in the schemes of work. There should be a commitment to equality of opportunity and a cross-curricular perspective given in all schemes of work that should relate back to the whole-school aims.

Success

The pupils in any school have a right to experience success in their learning. For many pupils with special educational needs experiencing failure is the norm. Too often these pupils are judged by what they cannot do rather than what they can do. Another form of presentation of their work, for example in an oral rather than a written format, is often preferable, producing a more honest performance indicator of the pupil's knowledge.

Match

Matching curriculum work and curricular expectations to pupils' differing pace, style of learning, interest, capability and previous experience should be at the centre of any worthwhile scheme of work. Allocation and prioritisation of time and resources must be taken into account in matching the curriculum delivery to the individual needs of the pupil. Overall, the work which they are asked to do must match pupils' needs and appear purposeful to them. Various methods of working can assist in this matching of curriculum work to the individual needs of the pupil, one of which is peer tutoring (Bland and Harris 1988). There is notably a match between pupil and task but also between an able pupil and a pupil having special educational needs. Verbalisation, rationalisation and internalisation of the work being undertaken are greatly enhanced and the scheme can provide enormous benefits to all. An interesting development is the progress made by able and gifted pupils by this mode of working (Welch 1987).

Small achievable steps

For those pupils with learning difficulties it should be possible to break down the work into much smaller and more achievable steps. Instructions for specific tasks should be clear and brief with effort being rewarded as highly as achievement. Clearly defined objectives are required which the teacher can share with the learner. These should be expressed in terms of what is to be achieved, why it should be achieved and how it is to be achieved. Targets should be set which are short-term and easily attained. These require the teachers to be very clear about the knowledge, concepts and skills that are needed in any particular topic.

Expectations

Pupils have expectations of their work that may be higher than those of their teachers. Conversely too high an expectation by the teacher can produce difficulties for many pupils. Somewhere in the centre of this dilemma has to be an awareness of the needs of pupils. Under-expectation in the past needs to be coupled with a realisation of the extent of their capabilities, for example in identifying the knowledge which they bring to a task, as outlined by Hackett (1989).

Communication methods

Flexibility and a range of alternative strategies are imperative in differentiating and communicating. The majority of pupils with learning difficulties can access the National Curriculum if the method of communication is tailored to their needs. It is important to recognise that some learners will require additional support in order to communicate their findings in a manner that gives them every opportunity to express what they know and understand. Traditionally, the written outcome of the learning task has often been viewed as the indicator of understanding and progress. Other modes of communication, for example word processor, tape recorder, video, etc., highlight the process undertaken rather than the end product.

Pupils' perceptions

Pupils' own perceptions are often an untapped resource and interactions between the teacher and the pupil should generate an atmosphere in which the pupils' perceptions can be voiced and understood. Will the purpose of the activity, and the method employed to achieve it be understood and enjoyed by the pupils? Children bring with them experiences of learning that are not necessarily school-orientated. These experiences emanate from their daily lives and can lead to a very different perception of school and the school tasks being asked of them. Pupils often fail to make the conceptual links between the task as presented at school and tasks in the real world. For example pupils working mathematically at ratio in the classroom often fail to see any real connection between amounts needed for mixing mortar in the everyday world.

Cross-curricular themes

Much has been written about the involvement of all subject areas during the planning stage of curriculum development. Primary experience has tended to utilise this method of delivery far more than secondary provision. Early examples of cross-curricular themes in primary schools were to take the National Curriculum science topics and ensure that all other foundation subject work from maths and English emanated from it. With other subject areas, for example history and geography for which the statutory instruments are now published, there is a widening of topic choice which leads to a much more balanced cross-curricular topic web being produced.

Although published before the introduction of the National Curriculum, the study by Klotz and Cowne (see Chapter 9) is a good example of a cross-phase, cross-curricular project. Its content covers much of the subject matter in Key Stage 2, Programme of Study for History, Core Study Unit 1. This is concerned with Invaders and Settlers, 55 BC to 11th century AD. Similarly, it encompasses skills from Key Stage 2, Programme of Study for Geography in the areas of Geographical Skills, Places and Themes (local area), Physical, Human and Environmental Geography.

Secondary colleagues could facilitate the responsibility for certain curricular areas being taught by specific departments, in order to be more cost-effective on teacher time. Particular areas, for example personal and social education, must have an all-pervading cross-curricular theme if the scheme of work is to achieve any form of success. Work covered under the pastoral umbrella must relate to work done in the academic sphere and whole-school policies have a large part to play here in the delivery of cross-curricular working to pupils.

Resources

Schemes of work should be drawn up with reference to the resources currently available and with due consideration having been given to financial implications. The resources that the pupils can bring to their own learning should be fully utilised. Children can be very resourceful and can adapt and utilise materials in many ways if encouraged to do so. An example of this was a scheme organised by pupils who collected petrol tokens from their parents in order to exchange them for cassette tapes and Walkmans. Texts from popular published mathematics schemes were then recorded, thus enabling a pupil with reading difficulties to access what was being asked of him/her mathematically without being hindered by difficult text. Mixed ability teaching situations and differentiated group work are often more resource-based than other teaching situations. Children progressing at different rates, will be less dependent on the teacher but more heavily dependent on appropriate resources and materials being readily available. There needs to be whole-school collaboration on resources, their cost implications and organisation in order that they can be effectively deployed over a wide range of learning situations.

Teaching and support staff

The deployment of teaching staff, support teachers and non-teaching staff will have a marked effect on the implementation of schemes of work. A whole-school policy on the provision for pupils with special educational needs should match teacher strengths to pupil needs and allow for continuing staff development throughout the school. Personal practice and styles of teaching should be constantly under review.

Recording progress/celebrating success

When recording pupils' progress within National Curriculum guidelines there needs to be school-wide procedures for the reviewing and evaluation of work. Record keeping is an integral part of the professional aspect of curriculum provision and is one method by which the teacher and child can celebrate success. Time spent on recording and evaluation leads to time saving in the planning and delivery of future teaching. Pupils' perceptions and explanations assist the recording of progress and provide indicators as to how learning took place. Records of achievement have greatly assisted pupils with special educationai needs by involving teacher and taught in the process of recording, enabling the pupils to voice their opinions and knowledge and the teacher to record that information in the child's presence.

Conclusion

One can identify the impact that the BBRDs and curriculum plans are having. Relevant and rigorous staff development and enhanced provision for pupils with special educational needs are appearing as necessary remedies to the previous malady. Ensuring that all pupils can gain access to the curriculum at their own particular level and make notable progress upon it is one of the hardest tasks to fulfil in curricular entitlement. Far better to recognise these problems and to work diligently for their solution than to have a group of pupils not working on the same curriculum as all other pupils in the country. Much has been done to establish responsibility for all pupils' learning firmly and squarely with the classroom teacher. No longer is it acceptable to pass on that responsibility to other members of staff interested in special educational needs or to those willing members of the peripatetic and support services. However many class-teachers are very concerned about their overall responsibilities and need varying degrees of assistance to enable curriculum access for all to become effective. Positive attitudes from staff along with home – school partnerships will assist the process. A learning environment conducive to warmth and support where pupils can feel self-confident and valued and not inhibited by fear of failure is a necessary precursor to success in the teaching of pupils with special educational needs. However broad, balanced, differentiated and relevant to the pupils' needs the curriculum on offer is, the relationship between teacher and taught is of paramount importance. How many times do we note successful learning situations when class teacher and class are in harmony, working together and achieving success? In these times of poor media coverage for education and its teachers it is imperative that the professionalism of teachers is not lost. However, the new challenges of preparing pupils for the turn of the century within the framework of ERA must be taken on board and standards of pupils' achievements should continually improve.

Little has been said in this chapter about the exceptional arrangements that may need to be implemented for some pupils. Only rarely should pupils require 'exceptional arrangements' for modification to or exemption from the National Curriculum and only then when it is deemed impossible or totally inappropriate for the pupils' special educational needs. The complex nature of the arrangements which have to be undertaken in order to exempt pupils from the National Curriculum will go some way to prevent some practitioners from abdicating their responsibilities. Although much of what is appearing as custom and practice under LMS may be seen as detrimental to provision for pupils with special educational needs, mention should be made that, under the majority of schemes submitted, finance could be withdrawn if there was a failure to show that there was satisfactory provision for children experiencing learning difficulties. This encompassed both policy and resources.

Thus in a period of change and of 'moving goal-posts', pupils with special educational needs still provide the challenge that they always have. They will continue to need the very best of provision. As the 1990s unfold further difficulties and complaints will emerge and rethinking will invariably take place. However, the starting point of a curriculum for *all* was the first hurdle of ERA. It remains to be seen whether the adjudication of its implementation is successful.

References and further reading

Barthorpe P. and Visser, J. *Differentiation: Your Responsibility*. Stafford: NARE.

Bland, M. and Harris, G. (1988) Peer tutoring as part of collaborative teaching in Chemistry *Support for Learning*, **3**, 4.

Hargreaves, D. (1982) *The Challenge for the Comprehensive School* London: Routledge and Kegan Paul.

Hackett, G. (1989) Let's write a story *Support for Learning*, **4**.

DES (1988) The Education Reform Act. London: DES.

DES (1978) Special Educational Needs (The Warnock Report). London: HMSO.

NARE (1990) *Curriculum Access for All*. Stafford: NARE.

NCC (1989) Curriculum Guidance 2: *A Curriculum for All*. York: NCC.

Welch, J. (1987) The individual needs of gifted children *Support for Learning*, **2**, 4.

7 Peer tutoring as part of collaborative teaching in chemistry

Mary Bland and Graham Harris

T.P. Riley Community School is a group 12 comprehensive school situated in the northern boundary of the Walsall metropolitan district. We are a split-site school, the first two years being based in buildings some three quarters of a mile from the main site. There are approximately 1350 pupils on roll. The catchment area is varied including areas of genuine material and social deprivation as well as pleasant private housing.

School curriculum and organisation

In 1985 a new curriculum pattern was introduced which effectively created an enabling structure providing teachers with a variety of ways of organising the content and style of their lessons and the composition of teaching groups. Years one and two are taught predominantly in mixed ability tutor groups. Thereafter some curriculum areas choose to group pupils by ability.

Provision for special educational needs

The enabling structure made it possible for the then special needs department, to work alongside subject teachers across the curriculum, age and ability range. The focus shifted from students' difficulties to the whole learning process — the teachers involved, their curriculum content and organisation, and classroom methodology.

Special needs now operates as a team of learning coordinators whose brief includes stretching the most able as well as aiding those with learning difficulties.

The aim is to ensure that the curriculum on offer is accessible to all students irrespective of their varying abilities so that each student can be offered a rich educational diet. The key factor is successful learning for all. The subject specialist sets the learning targets and the learning coordinators assist in providing the vehicles through which these targets can be met.

Skilling the ordinary classroom teacher: the peer tutoring approach

It is such a partnership which has enabled Graham Harris, Head of Chemistry and Mary Bland, Head of Learning Coordinator Team to try out an interesting American teaching strategy — namely peer tutoring.

Originally, the two authors spent six weeks in the summer term of 1987 exploring peer tutoring's possibilities, attempting to define its best application and modifying the technique accordingly. Science provided a good basis for this, since lessons constitute both practical and theory learning and a combination of student-centred exploration along with more teacher-directed learning.

In the autumn of 1987 we spent a further seven weeks videoing peer tutoring chemistry lessons. For purposes of comparison we filmed two third-year classes one of which comprised a mix of abilities but generally well-motivated students, the other a more challenging group containing reluctant and occasionally truculent students.

The science curriculum

Chemistry lessons ran for one hour per week. Work being covered during the summer involved the writing of chemical equations, a concept that had always caused difficulty for pupils meeting it the first time. The writing of equations is a concept built up over a long period of time, starting in year three by writing equations in words. Chemical symbols and formulae are introduced during the GCSE course. It was the surprising speed with which students rapidly grasped a notion, the gist of which had often previously taken several lessons and considerably more teacher effort to achieve, that convinced Graham Harris of the potential of peer tutoring in substantially improving the learning process.

In the autumn term, students were being introduced to the idea of elements and compounds. The use of peer tutoring seemed ideally suited to one particular task, that of following a series of rules in the naming of chemical compounds.

Preparation and organisation

Preparation for a peer tutoring lesson involves ranking the class list in order of ability in that subject. Students are then paired off, most able with least able and so on. If preferred, instead of simply giving students the name of their partner a learning exercise can be used, e.g. in a chemistry lesson, one half of the pair is given a chemical name, the other half the symbol for the chemical. In a geography lesson, match rivers, oceans, cities, etc. Students can then play a 'find your partner' game. If students are simply told whom to work with use colour coding, i.e. red for least able, yellow most able.

Method

The lesson begins with teacher instructions about the learning tasks required of students. This is followed by students working collaboratively with their partners at their first task. The teacher is free to check that each pair is successfully completing the task. The correct version is then used in the peer tutoring exercise. The least able (red) first checks out the most able (yellow) who this time perform the task independently. Roles are then reversed reds (least able) working independently checked out by yellows (most able).

Peer tutoring is most useful in the case of factual learning or when the teacher wants students to become proficient at a particular skill. Here is an example of a third year chemistry lesson:

Theory lesson — naming compounds

Students are paired off least able with most able

We used a learning exercise to introduce students to their new partner. Everyone was issued with a periodic table of elements, necessary for the ensuing lesson, which was labelled with either the name or the symbol of an element. With their periodic table of elements for reference, students had to seek out their partners, matching names to symbols. (The most able had names, the least able symbols).

Teacher instruction

The pair's atomic numbers matched a numbered bench in the lab which enabled us to control seating arrangements.

The lesson began with teacher instruction on the rules for naming compounds and an introduction to the first task, exercise 2 on the worksheet Naming Compounds (see figure 7.1).

Students work collaboratively in their peer tutoring pairs

Students initially worked together in their peer tutoring pairs combining their efforts for this first task, while the teacher checked that they were making the correct responses.

Teachers check students' responses

Having received affirmation, students helped themselves to the next task which was the same work presented differently. For example:

Match the contents of this envelope correctly

Zn S		Silver iodide
Mg O		Zinc sulphide
Ag I		Magnesium oxide

Students practise new learning testing each other out

The less able student, using the worksheet as a correct version, checks out the most able who this time must perform the above tasks independently. Then roles are reversed and the most able checks out the least able. Students performing the task may refer to their periodic table but the 'tutor' alone has access to the worksheet. Students continued through the worksheet, in their pairs, using the peer tutoring model to check each other's progress.

Peer tutoring can be used without elaborate learning materials

Although we had homemade materials to consolidate the learning on the worksheet available to students, we found that this can be done just as effectively by simple use of scrap paper and pencil, allowing students to devise tests for each other.

Practical experiments

It was previously stated that peer tutoring's best application lay in factual learning or skill-based learning, where the teacher wishes students to have certain knowledge at their fingertips before proceeding to the next stage of learning. It should be said, however, that we found students worked efficiently and accurately in their peer tutoring pairs while performing experiments. In this situation the least able but sometimes more confident or outgoing one of the pair took the lead and busily organised setting up the experiment while the more able partner made pointers towards accuracy or provoked a more considered response from their partner when it came to observations or conclusions.

Empirical evidence

Our empirical evidence, borne out by students' and teachers' assessments of this new classroom methodology as well as analysis of the record on film, indicates that peer tutoring has the following benefits.

1. Peer tutoring is simple and sound. It has the advantages of computerised direct instruction, in particular the dialogue between teacher and taught, but without the cost.
2. Students talk to each other instead of teacher using talk and chalk.
3. Students are well motivated perhaps because they have more responsibility for discharging their learning. The onus is on them to summon teacher's aid as they feel appropriate. They often prefer to tackle the challenge themselves first.
4. Students are continuously concentrating upon the task and thoroughly involved with their work.
5. Students' talk is centred on the work. There are no extraneous conversations, possibly because friendship groups are split and they have therefore only the work in common.

T.P. Riley Community School   Chemistry Department

Naming compounds

1. The name of any metal present in the compound
   always goes first.
2. Compounds containing just two elements always
   have a name that ends in *-ide*.
   e.g. Cu O   Fe S
   copper ox*ide*   iron sulph*ide*

Now try these for
yourself:

Mg O _____	Mg Cl$_2$ _____
Na Cl _____	Na$_2$ O _____
K Br _____	Ag I _____
Li F _____	Ca Cl$_2$ _____
Zn S _____	Al$_2$O$_3$ _____

3. Compounds containing more than two elements
   have a family name;

   SO4 is the *sulphate* family
   OH is the *hydroxide* family
   CO3 is the *carbonate* family
   NO3 is the *nitrate* family

   e.g. Cu SO4   NA OH
   copper *sulphate*   sodium *hydroxide*

Try these:

K NO$_3$ _____	Ag NO$_3$ _____
Ni SO$_4$ _____	Li OH _____
Zn (OH)$_2$ _____	K$_2$ SO$_4$ _____
Pb (NO$_3$)$_2$ _____	Ca CO$_3$ _____
Mg SO$_4$ _____	Al (OH)$_3$ _____

4. When two non-metals are joined together in a
   compound the name still ends with -ide but you also
   have to say how many atoms are joined to the single
   atom using:
   mono = 1 di = 2 tri = 3 tetra = 4 penta = 5 etc.
   eg. C O   C O$_2$
   carbon *mono*xide   carbon *di*oxide

Try these:
   P Cl$_5$ _____
   P Cl$_3$ _____
   S O$_2$ _____
   S O$_3$ _____
   C Cl$_4$ _____

Other important formulae   Try to remember these:

H$_2$ O	water
H$_2$ SO$_4$	sulphuric acid
H Cl	hydrochloric acid
H NO$_3$	nitric acid
H$_2$	hydrogen (gas)
O$_2$	oxygen (gas)
C H$_4$	methane
N H$_3$	ammonia

Make a list of any others you come across in the
space below.

Figure 7.1   Example of a worksheet used in peer tutoring

6. Pairings appear to work well. There has been, surprisingly, no grumbling from students about taking their partners, although we do use the 'rule, praise, ignore' approach to safeguarding peer tutoring in its inchoate stage. Students do not seem to comment on the ability matches even in some classes where we thought this was very obvious. Boys and girls appear to work happily together. In fact, the pairings have worked amazingly well, falling into a pattern of exchange over instructions, guidance and shared observations. Students are polite and considerate towards each other.

7. A non-threatening atmosphere is created for students to practise new learning immediately after it is introduced.

8. Instant peer prompting and correction enables pupils to proceed with their work thus avoiding the typical delay students may experience in waiting for teacher assistance.

9. Incidental instruction occurs, for example, one student correcting another's spelling.

10. The least able or less confident gets three bites at the cherry, so to speak, once from teacher's instruction, then from their more able partner and finally in having to work through the task themselves. Several previously reluctant students have blossomed in the peer tutoring situation, contributing just as much as their usually better motivated partner.

    Poor readers seem to cope with complex material which has been beyond them in a less supportive or less structured environment.

11. For both students, peer tutoring presents a concentrated learning experience. In performing it, they both verbalise, rationalise and thus internalise. Gartner, Kohler and Riessman (1971) in their research reported learning gains for least and more able alike.

12. Students can learn at their own pace and varying rates.

13. The implications for students developing effective working relationships could be significant in terms of their post-school opportunities.

14. Breaking the lesson down into a series of tasks gives pace to procedures and the classroom becomes a hive of industry. The general atmosphere is of a business-like nature.

    In this way, too, the teacher maintains instructional control. The strategy thus combines of child-centred learning with teacher direction.

15. Peer tutoring creates an heuristic element to the lesson, thus freeing the teacher to play the role of resourcer and listener. The latter can provide valuable indicators to future lesson planning.

Outcomes

In the early days, a couple of amused but obviously interested science teachers observed our antics from a cautious distance. Perhaps motivated by curiosity, they sidled off to split their classes into the most able, least able pairs and carry out a little informal experimentation of their own. They were quick to recount their experiences to us each describing marked improvements in students' attitudes, behaviour and most significantly in their learning. Lessons, which ranged from second years to fifth years and included in one instance the sixth form, were judged substantially superior in quality.

Peer tutoring has now been successfully used in the foreign languages, humanities and maths curriculum areas. It was the subject of a formal in-service training session offered to staff at T.P. Riley on one of our staff training days in 1988. It is also featured in an ideas booklet containing suggestions for alternative teaching approaches issued to staff by the learning coordinator team.

Reference

Gartner, Kohler and Riessman (1971) *Children teach children*, New York: Harper and Row.

8 Let's write a story

Gill Hackett

This experiment in collaborative writing developed in response to the needs of a group of children for whom writing was a difficult and tortuous process. They were members of a class of third and fourth year junior pupils and in spite of my attempts to provide a wide range of writing activities they appeared to find little satisfaction in their work.

The idea of writing stories for younger children is, of course, not new, having been suggested in *A Language for Life* (DES 1975) as one way of establishing a sense of audience in writers. I wondered whether working with others in a group to produce such stories would be a means of enabling my less able writers to produce a finished piece of work in which they could take pride. The work of the Assessment of Performance Unit (1986) states that there should be a definite purpose for writing and that work could sometimes be collaborative in the stages of both composition and revision. The Scottish Writing Project (SCOLA 1982) suggested that too many children did not understand the purpose of a piece of writing or where its difficulties lie. I felt that this was particularly true of my reluctant writers.

Stage 1 — getting started

I introduced the idea of the story project to the class by commenting that it was a pity that some of the stories they wrote were never seen or read by anyone but ourselves. I suggested that they might enjoy writing for the children in the infant classes. At first the reaction was mixed. Those who enjoy writing anyway were enthusiastic but the less able were clearly not so sure. One child asked whether the stories could be written up into proper books with illustrations. As this had been my intention anyway I readily agreed and at that point the reluctant writers became more enthusiastic.

Ideas for stories began to be suggested but I asked the class to consider ways in which we could find out for certain what younger children really enjoyed. We agreed that we should go to the infant library area and spend some time looking at their books. Before doing so we thought about what we actually wanted to find out. The children decided they needed to read some books to discover what kind of characters and stories were in them. They also felt they needed to examine the layout of the books, the proportion of print to illustration, size of print, vocabulary, sentence structures and lengths. This seemed rather a lot to do but all the suggestions had come from the class so we set off at once.

A most productive half-hour was spent examining books. Most of the children, including the less able, took the research very seriously and could be overheard conferring with each other about the various points at issue. Many came to me with observations, some of them quite unexpected. One boy noticed that there were no inverted commas for speech in the book he was reading.

'I expect that is to make it easier,' he remarked.

The library area contains a wide range of books for younger children, catering from beginners through to those with a reading age of eight or nine years. I suggested therefore, that children try to look at a selection of levels of difficulty and most managed to do this.

In our next lesson I asked the children to organise themselves into groups of three to discuss their findings and to try and select a class to write for. I chose three as the optimum number for the groups as this seemed likely to be better than two in promoting discussion yet not so large as to leave anyone without plenty to do. Friendship groups seemed to afford the best way of working, bearing in mind that while children will probably feel vulnerable about their own writing they might be able to accept suggestions from friends if what was clear in their own minds had not been made clear to the reader (SCOLA 1986). Groups were sorted amicably and choices of classes to write for were also made smoothly. The children about whose writing I was most concerned were conveniently distributed among the groups, each working with more able children.

After some exchange of ideas in groups we reassembled as a class. Many children felt that they still did not have a clear enough idea of what to write about and asked whether they could go to their chosen classes and ask the infants themselves what they would like. I had anticipated this suggestion and had already asked my colleagues in the infant department if they would be willing to cooperate in the project. Before the visits the children made notes of the questions they would be asking. They decided that if they asked merely, 'What kind of stories do you like?' they would probably receive very vague replies, whereas questions such as:

'Do you like stories about animals?' would probably be answered by just 'yes' or 'no'. They settled in the end for questions like:

'Can you tell me some of your favourite stories?' 'Do you like stories which are happy or sad?' 'What people/animals would you like in your stories?'

Each group spent twenty minutes in the class of their choice. The infants were all busily occupied in a variety of tasks and the older children moved around from group to group. This seemed to work well and as I went from class to class observing them at work they seemed to have no difficulty in making contact with all the children.

The return to our own class was a babble of enthusiastic chatter as they related anecdotes to me. From this point even those who initially were reluctant were now full of enthusiasm. Previously they had accepted my suggestion that this project would be worthwhile but now they were fully involved. They were overwhelmed with the number of suggestions they had gathered and spent some time in groups trying to decide how many of the strands they could weave together into a story. All groups came to the conclusion that they would have to be selective in their choice of characters and situations and useful discussions developed as they juggled ideas and began to venture the first outlines of their stories.

Story summaries

Bungle the Bear. Bungle's favourite food is honey and he will go to any lengths to find some. Unfortunately, when he decides to raid a beehive, he gets badly stung.

The Lion that lost his Roar. Little Leroy Lion asks lots of animals to help him find his roar. When he is all alone and frightened he finds that his roar comes back all on its own to save him.

Magic Monday. Johnny is sad when his tooth disappears from under his pillow but no present is left by the fairies. He doesn't know that a witch has taken it to use in a spell. All ends happily when the fairies return his tooth having also made it magic (see Appendix).

Magical Monsters. Dan and Sue have an adventure when their football disappears down a hole. They meet monsters and visit a magical castle before returning safely home.

Craig and the Strange Man.   After disturbing a robber, Craig is kid-napped and given some strange medicine which turns him into a robot. Unfortunately, whenever he is given a job to do, the robot gets it all wrong.

Rainbow-Fall and the Animals.   During a thunderstorm a waterfall appears outside Magic's house, which is all the colours of the rain-bow. All of the animals are changed into rainbow colours and a monster comes to take them back to Rainfall Land. Magic tries hard to keep the animals but they all finally disappear with the monster.

The Haunted House.   Tony and his friends want to join Mike's gang but to do so they have to spend a night in the haunted house. The mysterious happenings of the night only end when the house finally falls down.

The Animal Rainbow.   Mr. Fuzzywuzzy and his dog try to help their neighbours who have lost some of their brightly coloured belongings. The search leads them to Mrs. Cackle, the witch, who has been collecting items to make a rainbow. Mr. Fuzzywuzzy tricks her and returns everything she has stolen.

Jimmy and the Monster.   On the way home from school Jimmy sees a spaceship and is taken on board. After some adventures, he finds himself back in his own bedroom and wonders if he has imagined it but that night from his window he sees the spaceship taking off.

Stage 2 — planning a method of working

Planning an outline for the story involved a great deal of thought and discussion in which all children became involved. We spent some time as a class discussing the features of a successful story which groups could then use with their own ideas. The following elements were chosen:

1. The story needed structure — a good beginning, middle and end.
2. Characters, whether human or animal, must be real and appealing to the reader.
3. An element of humour was desirable.

With these ideas written on the blackboard for reference each group sketched out a very rough outline of their story and were keen to begin. I did not want to curb their enthusiasm but I was determined that all children, and particularly the least able should learn as much as possible from the writing process so it was necessary first to plan out a method of working. The children were already familiar with making a first draft, reviewing this and then producing a final copy. They agreed that the finished books should be their very best work so agreed upon working arrangements which all groups would follow.

1. Writing a first draft — the story written as it was composed by the group members. This could be altered as they went along if they wished.
2. First review — to improve the story as a story. This would necessitate referring back to the guidelines previously drawn up to see if they were being followed. It would also involve checking whether any parts were too long or too short or could be improved by better phrases or vocabulary. The final audience had to be borne in mind.
3. Second draft — the story in its improved form would be rewritten in preparation for the final copy.
4. Second review — this time everything had to be perfect so spelling, punctuation etc. would have to be checked. Sentence structures and lengths would be considered.
5. Final copy — at this stage decisions would have to be made about layout and illustrations and the whole story assembled into an attractive book.

Stage 3 — writing the stories

The first actual writing session was very animated and I was pleased to see that the poorer writers seemed as eager as others to begin. It was interesting to observe the different ways in which groups approached the task. Two or three of the groups began writing at once. They would pause, quickly decide what would happen next, compose sentences together and scribble them down. Several groups took much longer to actually begin their stories, preferring instead to try and plan their ideas in detail first. Other groups worked steadily, planning part of the story together then taking it in turns to do the actual writing. Two groups worked meticulously on the wording of each sentence, constantly discussing their choice of vocabulary and questioning its suitability for the age range of the readers. Every child was involved. The reluctant writers all held back from being the group 'scribe' at this stage but contributed fully to discussions and decisions.

First drafts

The writing of the first drafts occupied one lesson a day for a week with groups tending to continue to work in the same way they had begun, as outlined above. This meant that while several groups wrote very large amounts others wrote much less but with far greater care and attention to detail. Each of the groups which contained a weak writer experienced problems as the week progressed. A hitch occurred in the creative process. Ideas were running short and no one seemed able to get them going again. Each time this happened I sat for a while with the group concerned. I asked if I might read the story so far, then it was always easy to get them started again. It simply needed a few prompts such as: 'Why did he do that?' or 'I wonder what will happen to . . . ?' and the ideas began to flow again. We would then work together until the next part of the story became clear. The weak writers frequently had lots of ideas when helped in this way and simply needed encouragement to phrase them into suitable sentences for recording.

First review

As the first drafts were completed we felt it would be helpful to draw up some guidelines for carrying out the first review. We produced a checklist of eight items.

1. Is the story interesting and enjoyable?
2. Is there anything missed out which could be put in to make it better?
3. Is there a good beginning, middle and end to the story?
4. Is there any part which is not clear?
5. Is the story too long? If so, where can it be shortened?
6. Is the story too short? If so, what needs to be added?
7. Can you suggest any helpful words or expressions?
8. Is the story suitable for the age range chosen?

As I expected, the children found the review process very difficult, particularly the groups who had written long, rather loosely structured stories. To maximise the usefulness of the exercise, therefore, each group then reviewed the work of another. Much useful discussion ensued and all stories were adapted to take account of the suggestions received. The children came to see the importance of not phrasing their comments as criticisms but of trying to make them in such a way that could be understood by the writers, helping them to appreciate the need for alteration in the work, motivating not discouraging them (Marshall 1974).

Most of my own comments were made in discussion with groups as I did not want them to feel that they were writing solely for my approval. When requested to do so, however, I did write a comment on each first draft praising strong points and offering suggestions.

Second drafts

The writing of the second drafts of the stories was completed relatively quickly. Suggestions from the first reviews were incorporated and further modifications were made by all groups as writing took place. The task of writing out the story was shared between members of each group. While one wrote the others discussed and tried out ideas for illustrations. The reluctant writers usually managed to avoid being scribe but this seemed to cause no difficulties. The process of discussion and contribution of ideas seemed to be regarded by all as being equally important. This was very important to these particular children as their sense of ownership in the story was growing all the time.

Final review

When the second drafts were complete all groups were ready for a final review of their stories. Most children found this easier to tackle as they knew exactly what to look for. They understood that lapses in legibility, spelling, vocabulary and punctuation would create a barrier between reader and writer (Schools Council 1983). Those children whose understanding of the rules of language was not so well developed learnt a lot from the others at this stage and they could gradually be heard to contribute more. Groups which had worked slowly and meticulously on the first drafts now had far less work to do than others. Once again the children wanted to have their work reviewed by another group and performed the task for each other most rigorously. Some groups were still unsure that their stories were ready and asked me to check them as a final safeguard. I was reluctant to appear to be marking their work but I agreed to look at anything they were unsure of and worked for a short time with each group, mainly suggesting improvements in punctuation. These discussions were useful as the children now appreciated their relevance.

Assembling the books

After so much work the children were excited at finally being ready to copy out their stories. They re-read their stories, dividing up the text into suitable amounts for the page. Sugar paper was cut, on to which text and illustrations were mounted. For ease of compilation this was in folded sheets so that they could be interleaved. This meant that the final number of pages had to be in multiples of four. Much sorting and re-sorting took place at this stage.

It was clear to all groups that work must be equally shared and the children seemed to have no difficulty in dividing the work between group members. Children with neat handwriting chose to be scribes and did not grumble about the work involved. Some of these were children who had been reluctant to write at the earlier, creative stage but now felt able to do so. The most artistic children were urged to work on illustrations. In some groups a particularly gifted child drew outlines of pictures for others to colour in while a third wrote out the story. Clearly the feelings of joint ownership motivated them to contribute in the ways most useful to the group and not necessarily in ways which they might otherwise have chosen. The ability to work cooperatively developed substantially during the course of the project. The final task for each group was to design a cover for the book. In the discussion regarding layout, lettering and illustrations, children exhibited a wide knowledge of the format of books and took great care over assembling their own special story books.

Stage 4 — presentation and evaluation

I arranged a time which was convenient to my colleagues in the infant department when groups could visit their classes to read their stories. This was eagerly anticipated all day by the writers! We spent some time discussing how they should approach this new experience. They felt it would be a good idea to show the cover and read the title first, to read quite slowly but with lots of expression and to show the illustrations as they went along. I left it to each group to decide who should read aloud and most groups decided to share the task equally. The reluctant writers, for whose benefit this project has originally been conceived, were also among the weak readers in the class but they were enthusiastic to take their share in reading aloud. The knowledge that the story was partly theirs seemed to give them confidence. (See Appendix.)

The infants provided ideal audiences greeting all the stories with enthusiasm. Their teachers reported that the storywriters performed well, often adopting different voices for the various characters and moods. They also commented that the stories were well written and illustrated, had followed up the suggestions made by the classes and were suitable for the age group for which they were intended. The children returned to class well pleased with themselves. They seemed impressed by how well even the youngest children had listened to them and were proud of the approval they had received from the infant teachers.

Our final class discussion was designed to find out what the children themselves thought they had gained from the story-writing project. They all agreed that they had enjoyed writing in groups. When asked what they found most valuable their replies included:

— learning to work with others;
— discussing and sharing ideas;
— thinking things out carefully and being able to change your ideas;
— learning to listen to others and take notice of their suggestions;
— getting along with others;
— sharing the work;
— learning how stories are put together;
— thinking about the children the story was being written for and not ourselves.

Conclusion

As a class language project, collaborative story writing turned out to be a great success. My original aim had been to encourage the reluctant writers but I found that all children benefited from working in this way. Their own reactions to the project were all positive ones and at no time did a child suggest that he or she had found the work boring or tedious. All children, even the most egocentric, learnt something about cooperating with others and were gradually able to make concessions for the sake of the group. I found that the quality of the finished products compared very favourably with previous work in terms of a structure, subject matter and characterisation. They had also managed to keep the sense of final audience to the forefront of their minds. During the course of the project the children undoubtedly learnt a great deal about the process of story-writing. Although they had attempted to review and edit their work in the past they achieved much greater success when working collaboratively and for the first time seemed to understand the purpose behind the stages. Because they wanted the stories to be as good as possible for the infants they did not seem to mind the time it took to refine and improve them.

Those children who previously had produced very little written work were caught up in the enthusiasm of their group. Their ideas were considered equally with others and this had given them confidence. Without the pressure of writing they had been able to generate more ideas and as work progressed so the sense of joint ownership developed and each child seemed to have a real pride in the finished article. At the copying out, illustrating and compilation stages they had further opportunities to make contributions on equal terms.

Like all the other members of the class these children learnt to share ideas and skills. They felt themselves to be valued by the group and this improved their performance and their self-esteem. When the stories were read aloud several were singled out for mention as having read particularly well which was an added bonus for them.

An important factor in the project seems to have been that the writers had very specific objectives and a clear idea of the audience for whom they were writing and this proved to be the greatest motivation of all. I know these particular children are very eager to try again and feel they have learnt a great deal since the day I first suggested, 'Let's write a story'.

References

Assessment of Performance Unit (1986), *The Assessment of Writing* Windsor: NFER—Nelson.

Department of Education and Science (1975) *A Language for Life*. Report of the Committee of Inquiry under the chairmanship of Sir Alan Bullock London:HMSO.

Marshall, S. (1974) *Creative Writing* London: Macmillan Education.

Schools Council (1983) *Primary Practice*. A sequel to *The Practical Curriculum* London: Methuen Educational.

Scottish Committee on Language Arts in The Primary School (1982) *Hand in your Writing* Edinburgh: Scottish Curriculum Development Centre.

Scottish Committee on Language Arts in the Primary School (1986) *Responding to Children Writing* Edinburgh: Scottish Curriculum Development Centre.

Appendix

MAGIC MONDAY

'Up to bed,' said Johnny's dad.

'Oh,' moaned Johnny. 'Do I have to?'

'Yes, and don't forget to brush your teeth,' said Mum.

'O.K.'

Upstairs, Johnny started to brush his teeth. 'Ouch,' screamed Johnny, his tooth had fallen out. While this was going on a pair of bright green eyes were staring at him.

Unfortunately, Johnny didn't see them. He wrapped his tooth up, put it under his pillow and got into bed. His mum shouted, 'Close your window, Johnny,' but he didn't hear her — he was fast asleep.

At 12 o'clock after his mum and dad had gone to bed there was a tap at the window. A thin bony leg started to climb into the room.

It was a witch. She was ugly with black spots, which she called beauty spots, but they weren't really. She crept over to Johnny's bed, lifted up his pillow and took his tooth. Then she crept to the window and flew off on her broomstick to her cave.

At half past seven Johnny woke up and looked under his pillow for his present. 'Oh,' he cried, 'The fairies haven't left me anything, but they took my tooth.' He went downstairs for his breakfast and told his mum all about it. 'Never mind perhaps you'll get something next time.'

'Oh, but mum, I want something now.'

'You'll get a smack if you don't eat your breakfast . . .'

Johnny didn't realise that the fairy went back to her toadstool wondering who had taken it.

Meanwhile the witch was saying to herself, 'I've got all my things. Check them Steptoe,' (Steptoe was the cat). 'Meeow OK,' he said.

'One fairy's wing,

The eye of a Goswangla,

The pips of a lily fruit,

The leg of an Octopuss,

A blonde hair of a mermaid,

The toe of a Winckle's Wag,

One boy's tooth.'

'Right, I will tip them into the cauldron. Now for the magic words.

'Hubble Bubble Squeak and trouble,

Hirty bitty make me pretty. Kabam . . .'

The fairy was flying around wondering what to do when she bumped into a cave. She went inside and looked around when she noticed a shiny white tooth. She knew it was Johnny's tooth because it had toothpaste on it . . .

The witch slowly turned the mirror round then she remembered she had not looked into a mirror for thousands of years because she was ugly. She looked in. SHATTER! The mirror broke into a thousand pieces. She looked at the recipe and said, 'Silly me, I'll have to get my glasses fixed. It's one fairy not one fairy's wing . . .'

While this was going on the fairies got the tooth and flew away. By now Johnny was out playing by the ring of toadstools, where it was said the fairies lived. All of a sudden there was a whisk of air and there sat two fairies gasping for breath.

'Here you are,' said the fairy, 'your tooth's here.'

'Oooh! Where did you get that from? You didn't leave me anything.'

'Here's something better than a present,' they said and rushed away. When they came back his tooth had got his name engraved on a piece of thread.

'This will keep witches away from you. Put it under your pillow when one of your teeth fall out. It guards your teeth and only I can break the spell.'

As for the witch, she never became pretty and never gained another boy's tooth. Because every night fairies guard your bed and will vanish any witches for good.

9 The Settlers Project: an approach to curriculum linking

Ann Klotz and Elizabeth Cowne

Background

There is a potential chasm into which children can fall between primary and secondary school. This is true for many children, but most of all for those with learning or emotional difficulties. Children nurtured and known by one class teacher can easily become lost and bewildered on transfer to the secondary subject system, taught by an ever-changing group of teachers, none of whom can know either the strengths or weaknesses of their pupils in as much detail as did the primary class teacher. It is very difficult for secondary teachers to find sufficient time to prepare material which neither under- nor over-estimates the wide range of skills of their first-year pupils, and at the same time is seen as interesting and relevant.

The Settlers Project, described below, concerns one attempt to prepare such material and thus to bridge the chasm. It was carried out by one secondary school and its five feeder primary schools, in an Outer London borough. A problem-solving approach was adopted. All participating schools were asked to contribute their solutions to a hypothetical historical/geographical problem, concerning the anticipated location of some 200 Saxons who had to leave their own country and cross the North Sea to found a new settlement.

It was important that all the participating primary schools should have a common problem which lay within the general area of geography, this curriculum area being chosen because the secondary link teacher was the head of geography. The link teacher for the primary schools was one of the borough's peripatetic teaching support staff. The original work had been carried out while she was seconded onto one of the London Institute of Education's one-term courses for Special Educational Needs in Ordinary Schools (SENIOS). The course project required each teacher to develop a priority area, either in curriculum or policy for special needs, in their own school. Mrs Klotz was in a novel situation in that she had been asked to use the project as a way of preparing the ground for children with learning difficulties who would transfer to the secondary school the following autumn.

What were the particular problems for such children, and how could they be best helped, and prepared for the transfer to secondary school? What emerged at an early stage was that these problems were by no means confined to special needs children. Firstly, they were to do with organisation, i.e. coping with homework, timetables, kits and so on. The second area of difficulty was their ability to adapt to a number of different teaching styles and subjects, within one day.

The initial contacts with heads of departments led to a meeting with the head of geography, who was very interested in first year pupils, and invited Mrs Klotz to observe his lessons. Together they extracted those elements which appeared to need extra work at primary level to prepare pupils for the subject curriculum. The project that finally emerged is described below by Mrs Klotz. It began when the head of geography introduced the Settlers Project as a problem-solving activity to each of the 4th year primary classes. After that, the class teachers developed the theme along very different lines. The five classes covered a wide range of ability and family backgrounds, yet nearly all the children involved became engaged and were stretched by the project. The end result was an impressive display of work at the secondary school. It was generally felt to be a worthwhile enterprise, which could well be repeated and extended.

Preliminary work

In Spring 1987 my time was divided between the secondary school and six of its feeder schools. There was a teaching commitment in one of the feeder schools. Apart from that, time was spent with 4th year teachers and their classes, observing and helping where appropriate. In most of the schools we also tried out exercises intended specifically to prepare upper juniors for secondary schools. The class teacher at school No 1 attached great importance to cooperative and collaborative work within and between groups. We adapted Activity No 5 The Auction from Douglas Hamblin's (1984) *Teaching Study Skills* to elicit a discussion about the skills and attributes needed for effective group work. This worked very well and the class teacher's skill in chairing the discussion resulted in a more insightful attitude towards group work. The class teacher felt that this attitude was later reflected in the group work for the Settlers Project.

In two of the schools we also tried out some role playing exercises. One of these schools, school No 2, had the help of the borough's drama advisory teacher. The activities he undertook with the 4th years prepared them for video drama described later on in this article.

At school No 5 the class teacher and I had a preliminary discussion with the class about animal rights. A decision was made for all of us to collect information for and against vivisection. When this was received 10 of the children, including 2 receiving special needs support, prepared speeches for and against vivisection. These speeches were made after a morning assembly to the entire junior school. For the hour between morning play and lunch time that day any 1st, 2nd and 3rd year juniors interested enough in the debate were invited to the 4th year class room. During the hour's debate which followed, the class teacher and I forgot we were talking with children because of the maturity of their views, their expression of them and the way in which they listened to each other's opinions. I felt that the whole process of this debate reflected the teaching philosophy of the class teacher in the setting of high standards and in demanding individual excellence. This was later reflected in the work this class did on the Settlers Project.

All six class teachers were alike in being excellent and committed teachers who had good relationships with their classes. They had very different teaching styles. The development of good working relationships with all of them was therefore an unexpected bonus. These probably arose through the joint planning, execution and evaluation of the exercises whereby our roles as mainstream and special needs specialists were forgotten. While the exercises did not figure directly in the subsequent Settlers Project, I felt that the experience we had already had of working together contributed towards the project's success.

Meanwhile, at the secondary school participation in the 1st year geography lessons provided some valuable insights. A class discussion on why the Romans chose London as a settlement site revealed a general lack of understanding of the whole concept. This led to consideration of introducing the idea as a problem solving activity to 4th year juniors.

One of the 4th year teachers had previously suggested that one way of strengthening contacts between a secondary school and its feeder schools would be for a secondary subject teacher to introduce a concept to a 4th year class, then to leave it with them to develop. The children could then present work resulting from this at the secondary school. A problem solving activity such as choice of settlement site seemed ideal for this. The second half of the summer term also seemed an excellent time for such an activity.

When the idea was suggested to the six feeder schools, one of then could not fit the project into the summer term's curriculum. Another was already involved in an interesting project but agreed to take on the Settler's Project as a subsidiary one with the proviso that they would not be able to devote much time to it. The other four classes were willing and able to devote a large part of the second half of the summer term to the work.

Implementation — preliminary resources

1. A map was devised. The area was very loosely based on the Thames estuary and divided into four parts, one for each school. A number of A4 copies of each area was made but there was also an A3 one for each class (see figure 9.1).
2. Our problem was divided into five stages borrowing very freely from Jon Nichol's excellent book *Evidence — The Saxons*. It concerned a hypothetical tribe of 200 Saxons forced to leave their home country because of flooding and fears of invasion. They had four boats, many women and children and old people, and animals and household goods. How do they plan the journey over the North Sea; choose their site, build their settlement; allocate jobs? Accompanying this was a set of teacher's notes giving background information on the Saxon way of life (see figure 9.2).
3. A supply of history books on the Dark Ages was obtained from the school library service.
4. Some preliminary information and work sheets were devised on the crossing of the North Sea, Saxon clothes, warriors, food and drink and social order (see figure 9.3).

Action

Two preliminary meetings were held to introduce the primary and secondary staff to each other and to distribute the maps, books and

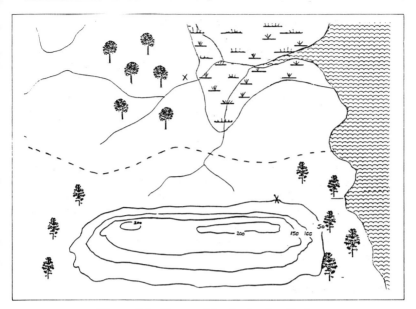

Figure 9.1 Map used in the Settlers Project

background information. Dates were made for the head of geography to introduce the concept to each class. Already, class teachers had very different ideas about how they would develop the project. The preliminary talks to each class were similar. The reasons for the Saxons leaving their homeland and the sea crossing were briefly described. The class then looked at the map and discussed what the settlers would be looking for in a site. I was present at the introductory talk at school No 4. Seats were placed in a semi-circle similar to the arrangement in a lecture theatre and 60 3rd and 4th years listened raptly for about 20 minutes to the introductory talk.

Afterwards, we divided into three groups to discuss which point on the map would be best for a settlement site. My group took it very seriously — thinking of the need for access to salt and how the type of soil would affect the kinds of crops which could be grown. When we reassembled and a spokesperson for each group gave reasons for their choice of site it was clear that the other groups had been equally thorough and wide-ranging in their discussions. Apparently, the introductory talk was equally successful in the other four schools motivating and engaging children throughout the ability range. Beneath is a brief description of how each school handled the project and the role of the support teacher.

Settlement Project – Background Information

From the first half of the 5th century until 2nd half of the 11th century, England was invaded and peopled by the Anglo-Saxons, a farming people driven from their homes in Northern Europe because of flooding and invasion by tribes from Central Asia.

England was largely defenceless. Invaders entered by rivers of the East Coast – the Humber, Wash and Thames. Warriors in boats holding about 40 of them would find suitable areas for settlement and would then be followed by farmers and families who would bring everything they owned

They found

River valleys with oak and ash forests
Beech woods on chalk downs
Vast salt marshes
Heather covered moorland
A network of well built roads falling into decay left by the Romans
The remains of Roman towns which scared them because of the size of the buildings, they called them giant towns

They needed

Access to water
Woodland
Cultivable land i.e. soil which wasn't too heavy

They had to avoid

Waterlogged land
Hostile neighbours

The Saxon Settlement

1. Britons would be killed or chased away from an existing settlement
   or
   Land in the middle of a forest would be cleared by burning and chopping down trees
2. Defend settlements with water filled ditches filled with earth topped with high wooden fences with sharpened points
3. Make houses from wood, wattle and daub (mud mixed with chopped straw)
4. Build a number of huts grouped round a central hall

Real fears

Saxons lived in constant danger from:
   Neighbouring settlements
   Gangs of thieves who roamed the forests
   Wild beasts – wolves, bears, wild boar, foxes, even lions
   Invading Vikings

Figure 9.2 Background information

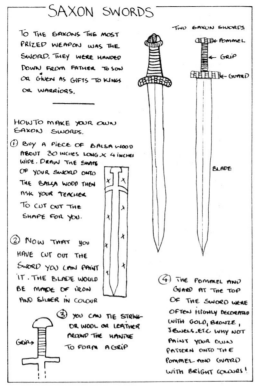

Figure 9.3   A sample worksheet

School No 1

This school is situated near a council estate and seems to be on an island surrounded by busy main roads. It has a predominantly working-class intake. Many of the children come from 'problem' families but are quickly absorbed into the happy and lively atmosphere of this small school.

There was only one 4th year class of 25 children. Seven of these received special needs support. The class teacher was also the deputy headteacher. For the project he divided the class into four groups. Cooperative and collaborative work within groups and within the class had been actively encouraged throughout the year. Following this philosophy, there were group decisions about the siting of the settlement and the journey from Saxony. The groups produced books describing the journey where each child had contributed their particular expertise. There were examples of weaving, paintings visualising how different areas of their map would have looked, model swords, shields and helmets, pictures of Saxon warriors and women. A detailed relief map of the area was made to scale and blown up to A1 size. A larger model of the settlement was also produced. Some maths was covered as work which had already been done on scale was extended quite naturally into the project, looking at distances covered by the map, discussing how large an area it would cover in relation to the size of the school and so on. The project took up the greater part of the second half of term and engendered a great deal of interest and enthusiasm.

The support role

There were only two visits during the project. The first time was at the beginning when the whole class was discussing the journey over and the siting on the settlement. They also discussed how various parts of the map would have looked. I had provided some extra reference books and because of my recent reading up on the period played the role of visiting 'expert' trying to answer wide-ranging questions on the Saxon way of life. The second visit was towards the end of the project and involved helping to make model swords. On both occasions I did not specifically support the 'special needs' children but gave help where it seemed appropriate.

School No 2

This is a nursery, infant and junior school situated near a large council estate between a busy main road and the river. It is a very caring school which also houses a playgroup and a children's centre with latch key, day care and holiday play schemes. Like school No 1 a number of the children come from 'problem families' but became absorbed happily into the calm and friendly atmosphere of the school.

There were 24 children in the one 4th year class. The class teacher was also the deputy headteacher. Four boys received special needs support. This class made four relief maps of their area and a number of pictures of how they visualised the settlement. The class teacher started the project by discussing how it feels to move house or school. One of the boys had been one of the Vietnamese boat people and talked about his experiences. This was a particularly appropriate way of leading to the concept of transition.

The highlight of the class's project work was a video filmed and photographed by the head of reprographics from the secondary school and some of his fourth year pupils, directed by the borough's drama advisory teacher. Here, the children role-played a film crew making an educational film about a tribe of Saxons looking for a suitable site within the area they had been given. One of the girls played the historical adviser; the rest of the class were the actors. The advisory teacher was the director. We used the device of a double suspension from reality. The children in their role of actors, played settlers as a means of rationalising the presence of the video crew and also any discussions they might have during the course of the action. The children incorporated what they had learned about the Saxons' pagan beliefs and culture to produce an improvised drama in which the whole class was totally involved. Every now and then the class was drawn together for a discussion about what they were doing, also for some advice from the 'historical adviser'. On the whole the children worked independently, cooperating to produce their drama.

The support role

No classroom support was given during the project. Instead appropriate work sheets were devised and I played a liaison role, putting the class teacher in contact with the drama advisory teacher and the secondary school staff.

School No 3

This school comprises nursery, infant and junior schools. There is a council estate behind it but apart from this it is situated in a pleasant and affluent suburban area. Reflecting this the intake is a mix of middle class and working class children.

The 4th year class only had 17 children, 12 of whom were boys. Four of the boys received special needs support. The class was already committed to another project so was not able to devote much time to the Settlers. After the initial introduction the class teacher suggested that anyone interested enough should devise a Saxon game. The reason she suggested this was because many of the children in this class enjoyed 'Dungeons and Dragons' type games and there were also quite a few Tolkien fans in the class. Two groups of boys volunteered and the 'teacher's' notes were handed over to them along with the reference books. One group of mainly bright boys began an incredibly elaborate role playing game involving, among other things, a lot of research on weapons. As well as the original four warlike and fertility gods they added gods of wisdom and peace. Unfortunately the game proved too elaborate to finish on time. The other group of boys, which comprised three able boys and two of those receiving special needs support, devised a game called 'Saxon Olympics'. This was a cleverly thought out game of dice throwing beautifully produced on a word processor. It has since been played and enjoyed by adults.

The support role

I only visited here once during the project just as the 'Saxon Olympics' was nearly finished. The boys used me as a guinea pig. It was Steve, one of the special needs boys, who was the most effective in explaining how I should play. I also helped with the research on weapons the other group was involved with on that day. It was enjoyable for me but such was the maturity and self-motivation of these boys that support was not really necessary at all.

School No 4

This infant and junior school is situated in a large council estate from which it obtains almost all its intake. Of all five schools involved in this project it has undoubtedly the largest number of special needs and problem children.

We had doubts about how appropriate the project would be because many of the children were not easily motivated and had short attention spans, also because the 3rd and 4th years were vertically grouped together. One of the three top junior classes had already prepared a project for the summer term but the other two very courageously said they would give 'The Settlers' a try. The project began very well as previously described. Apart from maths and science 'The Settlers' covered the whole curriculum for a few weeks. One of the class teachers was extremely interested in the Dark Ages herself and had a friend who was an archaeological illustrator. They very kindly made some additional work sheets for us. Her enthusiasm communicated itself to her class. They made replicas of Saxon shields out of balsa wood, helmets and pottery houses and marvellous model of a settlement. Paintings of the settlement and river and books telling the story of Beowulf were also produced. In the other class, a beautiful model of a keel was made in one afternoon's intensive work by Jason who had previously been unable to concentrate for much longer than ten minutes on any one task. Lawrence, another boy with learning difficulties, designed his own version of the Sutton Hoo helmet and had a heated discussion with me over whether or not Saxon boats had decorated prows. The project culminated in a visit to the Sutton Hoo Exhibition at the British Museum.

The support role

This was the school where I taught two days a week, therefore my involvement was much greater than at the other schools. At first, on the days that I visited the school, we divided the two classes into three mixed ability groups and took a group each for an hour or so. However, this was not practicable. Due to their growing enthusiasm for the project, my group became involved in work with their own classes when I was not there. I then gave support in the two classes as and when needed. Mostly, the support took the form of helping with language work or in giving historical advice. It was an insight seeing children whom I had previously withdrawn now working in the class situation. I continued withdrawing them for help with literacy but was now able to devise work which complemented and extended the work they were doing in class.

School No 5

This school is situated just off a busy high road. It incorporates a nursery, infant and junior school. There is also a Social Services' Under Five Unit integrated with the nursery, in addition to two units for upper and lower juniors with learning difficulties. Within the mainstream classes, children from troubled backgrounds and those with learning difficulties work side by side with bright children. Many of the latter come from literate middle class homes and were going on to independent secondary schools. This school absorbs all these diverse abilities and backgrounds so that at first glance the children appear as a homogeneous group. The atmosphere is a happy and stimulating one. A lot is expected of these children and they respond accordingly.

There were 25 children in the one 4th year class. Two of them received special needs support. The class also included other children with potential learning or behavioural difficulties and one girl who had recently been integrated from the unit. There were also a number of extremely bright and articulate children.

The class teacher wanted each child to produce at least one piece of work on the Saxons. By a delicate process of class discussion and talks with individuals and groups she set them all to work in many diverse directions. The result was a treasure trove of work which included a beautifully produced and thought out front page of a newspaper warning the Britons of the Saxon invasions and pottery models of Beowulf's dragon. The standard of work was high whether from 'special needs' or 'bright' children.

The support role

I supported for two days here. I sat out in the corridor and during the course of the two days the whole class was sent out to me whether as individuals or groups for help with whichever stage they were at in their project work. The class teacher made sure that she knew exactly where each was 'at' when they left me. Altogether the enthusiasm and wide ranging curiosity of the children made this an extremely enjoyable and challenging experience. Two children from the unit were also included and with individual help and support were able to produce work of the same standard as the mainstream class. This experience reinforced the feeling I had had before, that team work between mainstream and support teachers need not take place in the same room. I rarely ventured into the classroom and yet the class teacher and I were cooperating to the fullest extent in that we planned and evaluated the project together.

Initial assumptions

The Settlers Project involved about 150 children mostly, but not all, 4th year juniors. An implicit assumption was made that they were all functioning both conceptually and at a skills level of at least that of a 2nd year junior. In other words, they had some understanding of the purpose of maps; some notion of historical time and could trace if not draw. Some reading and writing ability was desirable but not essential. They could have coped without, and some did. At the top end of the ability range, no assumptions were made. Adult texts were available and were read intelligently. Where interest was expressed in a particular aspect of the project, we did our best to supply the necessary information and support. Some of the work produced was far beyond the standards generally expected of 11 year olds.

What was so special about the Settlers?

As mentioned before, the idea was borrowed and adapted from the Jon Nichol's *Evidence — The Saxons* (1979). Doubtless, countless primary projects have been based around similar problem-solving exercises. The books we used were the usual ones. The work sheets we designed were attractive and, we think, nicely thought out (we could all see a lot of room for improvement and extension of these sheets). We have all seen impressive displays of work resulting from the care, thought and imagination a good junior teacher will put into a project. The following points seemed to be special about the Settlers Project:

1. the involvement of a secondary subject teacher, drama adviser and support teacher;
2. the initial planning and organisation which freed the class teachers to concentrate fully on their own particular interpretation of the project and the individual needs of the children;
3. a cluster of feeder schools doing the same project in cooperation with staff from a secondary school helps to foster communication and continuity between schools which should ease the transition for those with learning difficulties.

The above factors resulted in the enthusiasm for the project of the teachers communicating itself to the children. Because of the unusually wide range of different kinds of work being produced, one was not often aware of dealing with special needs children. Instead, we found ourselves teaching children of differing cognitive styles and skills. By no means did the bright children tackle the written work while the slower ones did the art work. It transpired that the slower ones who wished to do written work were given support and guidance on the technical aspect of writing whilst the more literate ones were encouraged to elaborate and extend upon original ideas. Similarly with art work, help was given when and where it was needed. The end result was that the final display of work did not have a single piece of art or written work which had simply been copied from a textbook.

The initial objective

Were the initial objectives of this project fulfilled? Were children with learning difficulties helped in their transition to secondary school? We think that secondary and primary staff working together during the final part of the summer term led to greater mutual insight and understanding which would lead to greater continuity between the secondary school and its feeder schools thus easing the transition for *all* children. Unfortunately, only one subject department from the secondary school was involved and there has been little opportunity for follow up studies. It would surely be worthwhile doing a similar project on a large scale and following through the children in order to see how they then cope with the secondary subject curriculum.

References

Booth, T., Potts, P. and Swann, W. (1987) *Preventing Difficulties in Learning: Curricula for All* Oxford: Blackwell.

Golby, M. and Gulliver, J. (1981) Whose remedies, whose ills? in Swann, W. (ed.) *The Practice of Special Education* Oxford: Blackwell.

Hodgson, A., Clunies-Ross, L. and Hegarty, S. (1984) *Learning Together* Windsor: NFER/Nelson.

Hamblin, D. (1984) *Teaching Study Skills* Oxford: Blackwell.

Nichol, J. (1979) *Evidence — The Saxons* Oxford: Blackwell.

Smith, L.M. (ed.) *The Making of Britain — The Dark Ages.* LWT4, A Channel 4 Book, London: Macmillan.

Stenton, F. (1971) *Anglo Saxon England* London: Clarendon Press.

10   Support in action: the future of support services

Gerry Lewis

Introduction

Those who work in Special Needs Support Services have one aim, namely that they are out to make themselves redundant. In the present political climate that reality might come earlier than expected. Clearly this aim needs explaining. The support teacher undertakes a variety of roles within the school but the outcomes remain the same:

— that the pupil makes such progress that no additional teaching is needed;
— that the class/subject teacher acquires the skills, knowledge and expertise to deal with the problem him or herself, or can turn to someone in the school who is able to provide that needed advice and time;
— that the school has ensured its policy is able to accommodate the wide range of learning differences its pupils have;
— that the school has access to appropriate resources and uses them flexibly;
— that the school engenders an ethos and a commitment to take on these challenges effectively and efficiently;
— that the school is able to deliver a similarly high quality input as the support teacher has provided.

Only when all these conditions have been met and there is a guarantee that they will be continued indefinitely irrespective of future staffing changes and budgetary constraints, then and only then, should the support teacher willingly accept redundancy. What he or she will then do is set up as an educational consultant so that he or she can provide the necessary INSET that the school will need and produce the appropriate resource packages to supplement this work.

Quality

The support teacher has to offer a quality service. Without this central ingredient any kind of future is surely doomed and schools will quickly seek out alternative sources. It also has to be a service that is relevant to the school needs. Schools' expectations about what can be delivered have to be realistic and what is to be offered will need skilful negotiating.

However:

If support teachers are alert to the possibilities within their role, and allowed the flexibility to operate at the individual or whole-class level, then support for individual children can offer a way through to improving the quality of learning for all.

(Hart 1986)

Referrals

When asked to specify the child's problem, teachers often reply with fuzzy, general statements like, 'a spelling problem'. When asked to describe the action they had taken they might reply, 'have asked you to come in'. In order to improve upon this a referral form is often used which in addition to the usual personal background details also attempts to extract as much relevant additional information as possible:

— language spoken at home;
— date of admission;
— attendance over the last two terms;
— what the areas of current concern are — prioritise;
— what action the school has taken and its outcomes;
— what teaching programmes have been tried;
— how much time have been spent on them;
— what standardised test results (and SATs) are available (named and dated);

— is there any suspicion of medical, sensory, physical problems;
— is the child the subject of a statement;
— what other agencies have been involved;
— what other information might be seen to be of help.

Because support time is an expensive resource it has to be used efficiently. The referral form, after appropriate discussion and INSET with the school by the support teacher, can develop comments which are more focused.

What is the current concern?

Difficulties with written language work:

1. spelling often erratic — common words misspelt;
2. copying written work — often contains multiple errors.

Samples of work attached.

Action taken with outcomes

— Using Look Cover Write Check method. This was successful when applied.
— Encouraging drafting at work.
— Teacher rewriting work in collaboration with child, child then copy writes (improves content, but still many errors when copying).
— Recently introduced Ashgate spelling list and associated activities (enthusiastic and enjoys the games).

The teacher has provided a useful amount of in-house assessment and has also suggested her own depth of knowledge and teaching strategies. From that base line information the support teacher can now work with the child and teacher in a much more purposeful way. Little time has been wasted. Positive exchanges about different teaching approaches and resources can develop and the relationship between teacher and support is one of collaboration. The needs of the child, though shared, remain the responsibility of the class teacher.

Drawing up a contract

This will be of much more importance in the future because of the 'costing' or 'charge' which may be attached to it. Currently most contracts indicate:

— allocation of resource;
— type of intervention to be used;
— school action;
— evaluation;
— review.

The resource allocation deals with:

— direct contact time that can be provided by the support teacher;
— advice on specific or whole school approaches;
— materials.

To these are applied the following questions: 'When?' 'How often?' 'How much?' and 'How much will it cost?'

Intervention

There are two different support teaching approaches — the 'individual' and the 'whole-school'. The individual support approach encourages changes to the curriculum so that individual children receive teaching appropriate to their needs. It begins from the individually assessed needs of the child and attempts to produce a match between child and task. The whole-school curriculum approach examines the learning activity intended for the class as a whole and seeks ways of effecting change so that individual pupils can participate without being singled out. This involvement in general curriculum development work is of benefit to *all* children, but especially so for those with special needs.

The individual approach emphasises the progress of the individual child, whereas the whole-school approach is more concerned with teacher-awareness, teaching strategies and progress in curriculum development. Both approaches encourage in-class support in preference to withdrawal and both emphasise the need for curricular adaptation for children with special needs. By concentrating resources on individual children we may actually be missing the point. It may well be that the problems are more to do with the way the lesson is being presented, the resources and teaching strategies being used, or the demands being made on the child rather than with any specific problems of the child.

Intervening to help an individual

The type of intervention, if needed for a child, can be based upon dividing the teaching programme into small steps. This approach is not new. It is the way special educators have worked explicitly for a number of years and the way in which teachers tend to work intuitively.

Let us assume a child has a fluency and comprehension problem, and we wish to relate the programme to the child's regular reading textbook. The support teacher might devise the following sequence of activities:

1. Use key words from reading book in oral sentences.
2. Read new words from the book when presented in a sentence.
3. Read new words from book when presented in isolation.
4. Answers oral comprehension questions on sections of the book.
5. State the main idea of the book or part of the book.
6. Sequence events in the book when appropriate.
7. Predict what will happen next in the story — when appropriate.
8. Use own words to complete sentences.
9. Give definitions of words from the book.

When linked into the National Curriculum statements of attainment, another programme developed from the above could be expressed as:

Level 1   1. Invents a story when shown pictures.
Level 2   2. Expresses views based upon what has been read.
          3. Hears own mistakes in reading aloud and self-corrects with prompts.
          4. Offers sensible guesses, based on context, on unknown words.
Level 3   5. Uses appropriate intonation when reading aloud.
          6. Retells story sequence and plot.
          7. Discusses characters in story in an informed way.
          8. Tapes him/herself reading.
          9. Reads confidently to others in group.
        10. Self-corrects without prompting.
        11. Moves from literal to inferential comprehension.

The support teacher usually has specific teaching resources associated with such programmes. Though commercially produced materials are available, and the support teacher is knowledgeable about these, often purpose-made resources are provided for the child and the teacher. As a resource and curriculum provider the support teacher has a significant role to play.

The end objective is to ensure the child makes progress within the curriculum subject and that the class teacher has the skill to make sure the programme is delivered within the busy classroom. This follow-up commitment from the school is crucial and is written into the contract with specified times when the support teacher and class teacher can meet to discuss progress.

Intervention — whole-school

Increasingly the support teacher is asked to provide school-based INSET. In one middle school the priority was 'Guidance on worksheets'. This kind of specific task has whole-school spin-offs. Support staff are expected to be 'experts' in their own field as well as acting as change agents on general curriculum issues. Because their own experience and knowledge may be limited, support teams often get together to produce 'packages'. These contain the combined wisdom of the group. This can then be marketed in several schools and several support staff can then give the presentation.

In this example, the descriptors of a good worksheet were given as:

1. to cater for the full ability range found in the classroom;
2. to ensure objectives are specified and relevant;
3. to use appropriate language and reading levels;
4. to use a layout which is clear;
5. to contain diagrams/drawings of the highest quality;
6. to encourage the use of a wide range of learning situations;
7. to use a variety of resource materials;
8. to encourage active pupil participation to maximise motivation;
9. to review and have pupil feedback on the worksheet.

Further information and examples were provided for each descriptor. For Number 3, *Language and Reading*, it was broken down as:

Vocabulary is closely associated with passage difficulty. However, in many instances it is more appropriate to use technical vocabulary than to avoid it. Factors which influence reading difficulties are:

— size of print and print style;
— amount of information given on page;
— sentence length;
— over-complex sentences;
— unknown vocabulary;
— the number of 'difficult' pollysyllabic words used;
— frequency of technical vocabulary;

— extended, mixed use of personal pronouns;
— columns of print (too wide/narrow);
— frequency of new concepts/skills being introduced.

Support work has developed into broad and flexible patterns: from adapting or providing additional teaching materials for particular pupils, to cooperative work with the class teacher soundly based upon the assessment of pupils' needs, to that of INSET provider, 'consultant' in general advisory work, and curriculum development. The focus of this work remains centred upon meeting the individual needs of pupils within the classroom. It has also developed into the wider context of helping schools to organise their own structures and processes of management.

Support in action — the future

Many professionals now market the services which they offer. The importance of the customer to any enterprise is vital — after all, they have the money.

It will be increasingly important for SEN Support Services to:

— identify marketing needs;
— anticipate trends in demand;
— plan to supply acceptable products and services;
— be proactive in seeking new marketing opportunities.

To begin with there is a clear need to raise and maintain customer awareness as to what support services offer and do well. In order to develop this they will need to ensure:

— good contact with existing clients;
— to demonstrate that they do their job well;
— that the customer understands that the current contract was done properly;
— that all the essential information about customer needs is known;
— that future initiatives will be offered.

Support services need to recognise that they are offering the experience, expertise and skills of their own personnel and that the support teacher him/herself is his/her own best promoter. Like any business, staff will need to demonstrate:

— enthusiasm;
— expert knowledge of their particular skills;
— professionalism;
— initiative;
— integrity.

They will also be encouraged to make effective contacts with new and prospective customers.

1. It will be vital for support services to have clear 'mission statements'

. . . to support schools and colleges in meeting the needs of pupils in appropriate ways, taking into consideration the tasks, context and environment.

It may well be that this will have to be changed in order to accommodate for parents, and pressure groups like dyslexia. Once having been established 'support', can they always be sure of delivering?

2. There will be a need to develop strategies to win new contracts

With LMS, GMS and financial cuts this will be a vital development. Will support services have enough money to undertake this research? And will they be aware what the best strategies are? Will they be able to continue and develop those that already appear to work?

3. There will be a need to communicate effectively what support services offer

There is an important role to play with headteachers, governing bodies, parents, pressure groups and the LEA itself. It may well be that the current links with school need to be strengthened.

4. Support services may well have to rationalise what they currently offer schools

Perhaps support work is being spread too thinly at present. It may well be that services will have to examine closely their strengths and lose the 'frills'.

5. Support services will need to consider carefully what they do well

A 'shift' in current delivery practice may be necessary to accommodate what schools need.

6. Formal contracting between schools and support services will occur

7. There will be a reorganisation of support service staff on the basis of what the customer will pay for

It is likely that support teams will become smaller and of a more generic type, more multi-skilled.

8. There will be a need for support services to develop decision-making structures

New products and new markets will have to be found. There will be a need for these opportunities to be seized upon. Self-promotion will have to be encouraged in order to gain advantage over other similar services.

9. Support services will be used to monitor schools to ensure they are carrying out their statutory responsibilities

The forum of trust that has taken so long for support services to establish could disappear with this one move.

What is important to recognise is that the future of support services lies very much in the hands of the schools. It is to be hoped that they will continue to value them.

References

Hart, S. (1986) Evaluating Support Teaching *Gnosis*, Special Edition, 9 *DCLD Publications*.

11 Changing times: changing services

Phil Watts

Introduction

In these times of almost overwhelming change in education or 'innovation overload' as it has been termed, the first question that inevitably springs to mind is 'Do support services have a future?' As one who has recently taken on the job of heading a multi-professional support service my own answer is clearly 'Yes' (or why did I take the job?). The questions for me are: 'What do the changes mean for support services? What sort of future do those of us who work in support services face? What type of support will our colleagues in schools need in the new ERA? How will the changes in schools affect the type of support that children and their families require?' In order to address some of these issues this article will attempt to draw together the changes over the last ten years and to outline some possible implications for the future of support services.

The changing scene

For those professionals involved with children with special educational needs the last decade has been one of enormous change. This change has involved government reports and legislation, attitudes, provision, professional practice and organisation, and the development of new professional skills. These changes have been happening not just in the United Kingdom but in many other countries also.

In this country, the 1980s could be characterised by a number of trends arising from government policy and/or public/media opinion.

The emphasis on privatisation or the break up of large nationalised institutions and organisations, the trend of increasing central government control, the encouragement of consumer or market forces, and the development of an 'entrepreneurial economy' can be seen clearly in the face of British industry today. These philosophies have more latterly been applied to some of the major areas of responsibility of local authorities, both education and health. Within education, the last decade could be characterised by:

—   an apparent growing dissatisfaction about the process of education and its outcomes;
—   a shift towards the operation of market and consumer forces, with an increased emphasis on parents' rights, powers and responsibilities;
—   a lessening of the view that 'professionals know best' and to some extent a reduction in the perceived status of some professions;
—   a feeling that increased accountability of professionals and the institutions in which they work is needed;
—   an increased focus on the needs of the individual and the optimisation of the learning process for all pupils;
—   a reduction in the responsibilities and power of local government alongside the devolution of certain responsibilities to local level (e.g. local management of schools) together with increased central control over areas that were traditionally the province of the 'professional' (e.g. the curriculum).

These trends have been reflected by or translated into action by a number of pieces of legislation: the Education Acts of 1981, 1986, 1988; the 1986 Disabled Persons Act, and the 1989 Children's Act. There have also been a number of influential reports e.g. Warnock, Fish, Elton. The legislation and reports have all served to focus a great deal of attention on children with special needs.

It might be as well to remind ourselves that the term 'special educational needs' was relatively new at the start of the decade. The Warnock report (1978) recommended that the then current categories of handicapped pupils e.g. deaf, blind, educationally subnormal, delicate, should be replaced by a broader concept of special educational needs related to the child's individual needs as distinct from his/her disability. This change of emphasis, along with the emphasis on integration as apparently reinforced by the 1981 Education Act, has had significant effects on professionals working with special educational needs pupils. The emphasis for many support services has altered from focusing on the type of the child's difficulties (categorising) to diagnosis of exactly what the child's educational needs are (prescription) and how these could be met. It could be argued that this change has significantly altered the focus of many support services over the course of the last decade and promoted the growth that a number of services have enjoyed over the past ten years.

The timing of the 1981 Act and the Warnock report with their emphasis on the needs of the individual child, partnership with parents and integration, was not something peculiar to this country. There has been a considerable number of similar exercises in countries all over the world over the last 10-15 years. In the United States, for example, there are now a large number of states with 'mainstreaming' legislation. In Sweden most children with special needs are educated in ordinary schools or in attached units. In Italy the law providing for the integration of disabled pupils into mainstream schools was enacted in 1977. Many parents then withdrew their children from special schools, opting for the integration which the legislation aimed to promote. The effects there have been far more marked than here; the past decade has seen an exodus from the special schools which has forced the closure of many. In 1986 there were 100,000 disabled pupils (physical and learning) in mainstream schools out of a total population of 6.5 million. This response should be seen in contrast to the situation in this country where the response to integration has been patchy with some local authorities having reduced the number of children in segregated special education whilst others have increased their provision.

National Curriculum

The ideas of individual needs and integration are continued by the ERA legislation which establishes that all pupils in maintained schools, both mainstream and special, have an entitlement to a broadly based and balanced curriculum by law. It is not enough that the curriculum is offered by the school, it must be fully taken up by each pupil. The curriculum must promote development in all the main areas of learning and experience that are accepted as important and must develop the pupil as an individual, as a member of society and as a future adult member of the community. Whilst there are procedures for modifying or disapplying part or all of the National Curriculum for children with special needs, the DES appears to be anticipating that virtually all children will have access to it other than in exceptional circumstances. The DES publication *From Policy to Practice* (1989), a handbook about the National Curriculum, states:

In general, the approach which is being adopted is:

    — to allow as many pupils as possible access to the full National Curriculum — all foundation subjects, attainment targets, and programmes of study. The aim is to ensure that the wording of attainment targets etc does not raise avoidable barriers for pupils with particular kinds of disability or learning difficulty;

    — as a further means of enabling all pupils to follow the full National Curriculum without detriment, to modify the requirements to publish school-based information about the results of assessments but still assess how special needs pupils are doing. That way schools need have no fear that the overall picture of attainment for their pupils will suffer because pupils with special educational needs are included but such pupils can nevertheless benefit from the regular assessment of their achievements and future needs;

    — if necessary, to disapply or modify the assessment requirements, but still apply the attainment targets targets and programmes of study.

The message that is coming across very strongly is that children with special education needs are entitled to the same curriculum opportunities as all children and schools have a responsibility to deliver this. Indeed *From Policy to Practice* goes on to say '. . . No pupils should be deprived of access to National Curriculum attainment targets in mathematics and science on the grounds of disability' (DES 1989).

The emphasis in the National Curriculum arrangements on 'normalising' the curriculum for special needs pupils is likely to place significant demands on teaching staff in both mainstream and special schools. In mainstream schools these demands will be in terms of coping with wide variations in attainments in class groups and having the responsibility to deliver the National Curriculum at an individual level. 'Pupils *will* be able to work according to their own abilities and needs at each stage (of the National Curriculum)' (DES 1989). In primary schools it is likely that the National Curriculum will be delivered in a thematic or topic approach thus creating the need for clear observational, assessment and recording skills by the classroom teacher. In special schools the pressure is likely to arise from the necessary changes in the curriculum as pupils in these schools have traditionally received a modified curriculum according to their needs. These developments are, in turn, likely to be reflected to some extent on to the support services, whether it be in the form of increased concern over individual pupils' ability to cope or in respect of individual programmes, in terms of support in delivering the curriculum, or in work at the staff training/school development level.

The programme of national assessment will allow parents to judge the relative success of schools. Again this is an increase in public accountability and market forces if parents decide to use such information in choosing a school for their child. This requirement for testing of all pupils is in noticeable contrast to the advice of the DES' own Assessment of Performance Unit (APU) who, at the beginning of this decade, rejected the concept of blanket testing on the grounds of being too expensive, of being unnecessary for a good national picture and being positively harmful. They instead had recommended that a sampling would be sufficient. Exactly what effect the assessments and reporting will have on schools in respect of their special needs pupils remains to be seen.

The Elton Report on discipline in schools contains many recommendations that are likely to influence the roles and responsibilities of support services and teaching staff in schools, placing as it does much emphasis on a whole-school approach to discipline.

What is clear from this brief overview of special educational needs through the 1980s is that there has been an enormous number of changes initiated by central government and which have to be implemented at local level. To date, there have been significant changes in professional practice and organisation in response to these. The changes continue and we are only likely to appreciate the full implications of them for professional practice sometime in the next decade.

Changes in LEA funding and role

Changes in the role of the LEA were signalled in the 1986 Education Act which, amongst other changes, dramatically increased the power and responsibility of the governors of schools. Parent governors now constitute a significant number along with representatives of the local community. These changes together with the freedom of parents to opt for a school other than their local establishment furthered the process of local accountability and the introduction of market forces into education.

Further changes for the LEA are contained in the 1988 Education Act (ERA). ERA requires that school budgets are delegated to all schools with a population of more than 200 pupils, and local education authorities may choose to do so for schools with fewer than 200 pupils. The governors of schools again have a key role to play here — more local accountability. Additionally, there is a limit on the amount of money an LEA can retain for centrally funded services such as support teachers, psychological services etc. An

LEA can choose to 'delegate' (or it may be forced to because of its financial constraints) the financial responsibility for these services to its schools. Until 1993 the centrally retained fund is set at 10 per cent of the LEA budget (after certain exemptions have been accounted for); it then reduces to 7 per cent. This is likely to put severe pressure on some LEAs to delegate some of their services to schools. This means that school would be free to 'buy' in the services it requires. This may be, but not necessarily, from the original staff who were employed by the LEA to provide the service. This represents another extension of market forces into education. By now, no support service in the country should be left in doubt about its immediate future under LMS as all LEA schemes will have been submitted and approved by the DES. At the time of writing, the trend seemed to be that most services were due to be retained centrally as one of the discretionary elements — but what will happen when this reduces to 7 per cent? Will this be 7 per cent of a much larger base budget thus avoiding wholesale delegation? Will the 7 per cent be flexibly interpreted?

Working practices

This decade of change has left its mark in terms of the ways in which support services and special needs resources within institutions have changed and developed over time. Before this decade many support services focused their attention on the needs of individual children with an emphasis often being placed on withdrawal work; either within schools or to separate centres or clinics.

The realisation that these techniques were not necessarily the most effective and that there were a great many more children with special educational needs, as evidenced by the Warnock Report, that could not be helped by this approach led many professionals to seek other ways of working. A significant number turned towards an 'advisory' role, that is directing their support to those adults who had the maximum contact with the children, usually parents and class teachers. The growth of this approach can be seen in such initiatives as the Portage schemes for pre-school children and their parents which have seen most of their growth in the last ten years. Whilst Portage has been a great success, similar initiatives in schools have not always been quite as successful. Considerable attention has been given to the subject of supporting special needs pupils in ordinary classes and the general conclusions are that many mainstream class teachers experience the emotions of anxiety, fear, stress, worry and concern for the wellbeing of the remaining members of the class. They are also concerned about their own level

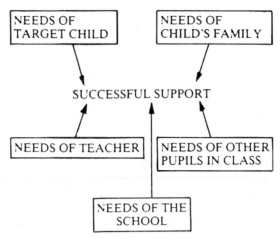

Figure 11.1 Factors required for successful support

of skills, knowledge and understanding and the level of support that they will receive from the support services. These findings and practical experiences have led many support professionals to seek ways of working that recognise these feelings and attempt to deal with the situation in a much more holistic manner than before. Successful support to special needs children depends not just on one of the factors shown in figure 11.1 but, potentially, on all of them and the interaction between them.

Support services have responded to this situation by initiatives such as 'in-class support', the rapid growth in in-service training, guaranteed time allocation from support professionals, etc.

Opinion of current practice

Before turning to our future, it may be a salutary experience to hear what others think of us and our services as opposed to what we think of ourselves. Both the DES, in its survey of support services, and local authority surveys have obtained views from headteachers such as the following:

— Support services were too varied in their style, delivery and quality of service. Too much depended on whom one had as one's representative.
— They were slow to respond to schools' perceived needs and sometimes appeared to put hurdles in the way.
— Assessment of individuals was slow and inconsistent between and within services.

—   There was much duplication of effort between services.
—   Schools were not consulted over changes in organisation, etc.

Does any of this sound familiar? Of course, from the support
service's side many of these points could be very easily reframed to
be a rightful part of a constructive way of working, e.g. 'putting
hurdles in the way' equates with 'following a Warnock model of
assessment'! Perhaps what is important is, not whether or not these
perceptions are valid, but that they are held by some schools and
teachers. These are our clients who could be offered the choice of
buying in our services or choosing to organise special needs support
themselves. What is clear is that we must devote a considerable
amount of time and effort to our customer relations and image.
Market forces are here to stay, at least for the time being, and
according to one well-known politician, 'You cannot buck the
market'.
    The DES also found that the support services which were
regarded *most favourably* were those that: negotiated their work with
schools; had a clear set of aims and objectives; made explicit to
schools what support was available; worked across age ranges in a
coherent and cohesive way; and had good links with other services.

The future

Special needs pupils should be a high priority for any local education
authority as it retains some statutory responsibility for them.
Circulars 7/88 and 22/89 allow an LEA to retain control of resources
for statemented pupils centrally, or to delegate them but to retain the
responsibility for monitoring and evaluating their use. Support for
special needs pupils should not be left to the uncertainties of LMS.
Therefore, based on a premise of equality of opportunity, it could
be argued that all children, families and their teachers should have
the right of equal access to support and advice from support services
irrespective of where they live, which school they attend or the
school's ability to pay. The implications of this are that support
services should be provided centrally or be co-ordinated by the
LEA.
    It is crucial therefore that the LEA uses its support services to the
full, making use of all the resources and skills that are available. This
could be enhanced by considering the levels at which a support
service can contribute to the education system and by having an
organisation that facilitates such an arrangement (see figure 11.2).
    In the light of the changes in the educational scene over the past
decade, it is perhaps worth considering a possible set of entitlements

Level 1 Working directly with children – assessment. teaching. counselling etc.	Level 2 Working in partner- ship with teachers. parents and other professionals to help children.
Level 3 In-service work and looking at organ- isation/curriculum in meeting children's needs.	Level 4 Advice to the LEA on policy, practice and provision. based on project work, research. marketing and evaluation.

Figure 11.2 Levels of work

for all the parties involved in support services work. The following non-inclusive list is offered as a starting point.

An LEA's expectations

As far as the LEA is concerned, a support service should:

1. work towards and fulfil a negotiated and agreed set of aims and objectives within the overall LEA framework;
2. meet its obligations regarding statutory work;
3. provide a negotiated and guaranteed level of support to all schools and other relevant agencies or institutions;
4. provide agreed and appropriate support and intervention for children and families that fall within the remit of the service;
5. provide information to inform and guide the LEA in its forward planning, policy-making and review procedures;
6. have clearly defined ways of reviewing its work and priorities, evaluating these and modifying the service delivery accordingly.

The clients' entitlement

Clients should be entitled to a service which provides:

1. a clear process for working in partnership in identifying needs, negotiating responses that draw on the full range of resources within the service and that respond to the client's current and likely future requirements;

2. a clear statement of the amount and nature of the support than can be offered;
3. support that, as well as meeting current needs, is proactive, enabling and developmental;
4. a menu of support that is available in order to inform clients;
5. named staff responsible for particular schools and other institutions to build up links and offer continuity.

The service's entitlement

A support service should be enabled by the LEA to provide a service that meets its aims and objectives through:

1. working at all stages of the Warnock model of assessment and at all levels of work;
2. making full use of all the available skills and expertise within the service;
3. the development of processes, materials and resources that support professionals' work and the skills to apply them;
4. the development of LEA wide initiatives and contributing to relevant centrally managed initiatives;
5. the continuing review of staff skills, knowledge, motivation and performance within an overall service development programme.

Staff entitlements

Staff within the support service should be entitled to have the opportunities to:

1. work at all levels of service delivery where possible and appropriate and to have access to a wide range of tasks;
2. work in teams with support being an integral part of their duties;
3. have personal interests and expertise included in service delivery whenever this is both practical and relevant;
4. have access to on-going professional development within a framework of identified training needs and a positively-framed appraisal system;
5. be supported by the management structure within the service and the LEA.

A possible way of working based on these entitlements is shown in figure 11.3.

It follows that support services must be fully engaged with schools

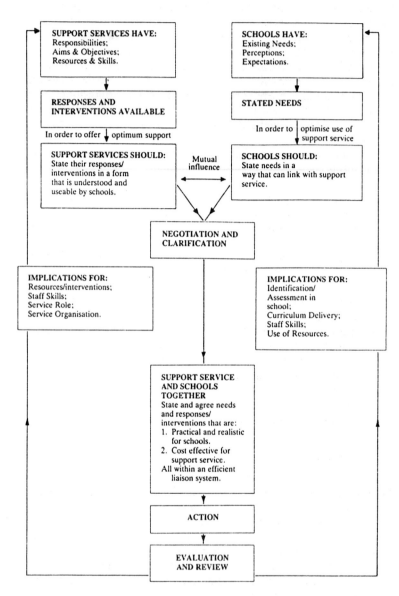

Figure 11.3 A liaison system between schools and the support service

to support them to deliver National Curriculum. This means that the focus of support services should inevitably shift away from one which is predominantly centred on basic skills and behavioural problems to a much broader view. Supporting pupils with special needs and their teachers will need to take into account their needs across the whole curriculum. This in turn has great implications for the way in which support services work and the skills which these professionals need in order to deliver successfully a service that takes into account the needs of the whole organisation — school, staff and pupils.

For support services to survive generally, the services they offer will need to be:

— *of high quality and appreciated by the consumers* — otherwise they will look elsewhere to private practices or they will seek to have control of the resources — 'We could do a better job ourselves!'

— *cohesive and coherent* — there is no room for unco-ordinated responses or for rivalry and/or overlap between different services. The LEA must present a unified front in approaches to schools and other clients. The choice is simple coexistence or no existence!

— *'owned locally'* — whilst the services may be provided centrally they must respond to local need at the level of individual school, family or pupil. It follows that they should be monitored and evaluated not only centrally but also locally in order that the clients know what they are getting, that they have some understanding of the various pressures, and a clear picture of the effectiveness of the service which they receive.

Conclusion

Support services can have a positive future if they adapt to the changing world of education and can draw on appropriate practice in the commercial world by having:

— a clear identity and a high quality product to offer;

— a marketing strategy, not just to 'sell' their wares but to find out exactly what the clients' needs and wants are and to be able to respond to them;

— an evaluation system that is an integral part of the service delivery and one which effects real change within the service when this is required;

— a full involvement with schools, not simply on a narrow

special needs front but on all the connected aspects and one
which offers a service at all levels of work;
— a full involvement with planning, monitoring and evaluation
   at the LEA level.

References

DES (1988) Circular 7/88 *Education Reform Act: Local Management of Schools* HMSO.
DES (1989) *National Curriculum: From Policy to Practice* HMSO.
DES (1989) Circular 14/89 *Education Reform Act: National Curriculum Modifications
   and Disapplication* HMSO.
DES (1989) Circular 22/89 *Assessments and Statements of Special Educational Needs*
   HMSO.
NFER (1981) *The APU: A Progress Report* Educational Research Memo 35.

Part IV
Management

12 A survival guide to time management and the management of meetings

Mike Hinson

> The thing to be done swells in importance and complexity in direct ratio with the time to be spent.
>
> C. Northcote Parkinson

Whether or not it is a manifestation of one of Parkinson's basic tenets, a general characteristic of school staffrooms these days is the high degree of harassment felt by teachers at the additional workload generated by the National Curriculum. 'It's only the second week of term and I'm absolutely worn out'; 'There aren't enough hours in the day, I don't know where the time goes' are just two of the remarks to be heard. Yet as agents and participants in change, if we want something to happen, we must allow adequate time and space for it to do so.

Setting up a time audit

The way to cope more effectively with an increased work load is to utilise working time more effectively. As a preliminary to considering ways in which this might be achieved, it is suggested that readers should keep a record of how they utilise their professional time for the space of a week, or even two. The discipline of keeping a time log is a useful, even salutary, experience for most people. The following basic procedure could be modified to suit individual requirements:

1. Using either a page-a-day desk diary or specially ruled sheets, divide the working day into convenient intervals — 15 or 30 minutes, or lesson periods.
2. Next, identify and list the most prominent activities in your working day. Obviously, this will vary according to your role. For example, if yours is mainly a classroom responsibility, your list will be different from that of the head of the pastoral care who has to allow time for home visits and interviews. For the sake of convenience, it might be helpful to allocate a code letter to each of these activities (see figure 12.1).
3. Note down the activities undertaken during each time period as soon as you can, together with the time taken. This operation takes less time than you might imagine. It is likely that, after a few days, you will begin to notice areas for improvement.
4. At the end of the week or fortnight, summarise the data under their respective headings. Total the amount of time spent on each and then work out the percentages of time devoted to each activity during the working week (see figure 12.2).

Code Letter	Description of Activity
T	Teaching
A	Covering for absences
X	Marking
L	Lesson preparation
E	Out-of-school activities
C	Courses
D	Duties e.g. playground
M	Meetings (you might decide to be more specific by adding additional code letters)
I	Interviews and discussions with parents, children etc.
P	On the telephone
V	Visits — work experience programme etc.
B	Break times
J	Travelling — as part of the job (e.g. peripatetic teachers)
O	Office work — here again you might wish to be more specific

Figure 12.1 Some suggested symbols for a time log

Reviewing the audit

Using the collected data, the next stage is to analyse and to consider
how efficiently you have utilised your time. In order to pinpoint
those areas which may need improving, answer the following
questions:

— Is the bulk of your time being spent on the main functions of
   your job?
— Has a significant amount of time been devoted to matters
   which detract from these main functions? If so, how could this
   be avoided?
— How much time is available for you to use at your own
   discretion? Could this be more effectively concentrated into
   one or two periods per week?
— Are significant amounts of time being devoted to routine
   matters or recurring problems which could be handled by
   another colleague or subordinate?
— Has this exercise highlighted activities which need
   streamlining? Would this be best undertaken in conjunction
   with other colleagues? (Have they carried out a time audit as
   well? If not, would this prove to be a worthwhile exercise,
   eventually leading to a pooling of ideas?)

CODE	ACTIVITY	TIME SPENT (TO NEAREST ¼ HOUR)	PERCENTAGE OF WORKING WEEK
T	Teaching		
X	Marking		
L	Lesson preparation		
M	Meetings		
I	Interviews		
P	On the 'phone		
A	Covering for absences		

Figure 12.2 Analysis of weekly time allocation

Planning your working day

Your time audit could well have been something of an eye-opener, therefore the next stage is to streamline the planning of your day. For this, first choose a record book with adequate spacing. This could be a page-a-day diary with hourly slots, a Filofax, or you could make up your own file using daily planning sheets similar to the format shown in figure 12.3.

Having entered the usual holiday dates, standing commitments and so forth, the remaining space can be utilised for time management. This is a vital part of coping with change.

Make out a list of what you need to do each day. Begin by establishing the nature of each of the tasks which need to be tackled, then arrange them in priority order. Adair (1988) defines a *priority* as being composed of two elements in various combinations, *urgency* and *importance*. He says:

> It is urgent that you have a punctured tyre on your car repaired, but it is not important. It is important that you begin to think of next year's marketing strategy, but it is not urgent. But it is both urgent and important that you convince the chief executive at your meeting with him at 4.30 pm about the new sales campaign.

This succinct explanation can easily be transcribed into educational terms e.g. next year's timetable is important but not urgent, whereas decisions to control unruly lunchtime behaviour could be regarded as both urgent and important.

As you prioritise your tasks, identify those which *must* be done today, as opposed to those which *ought* to be done today. There are others that can be left on the 'back burner' or delegated to someone else. Also attempt to estimate the amount of time which will be required to complete each task. Try to leave some flexibility, for example, time for the unscheduled visitor, or interview.

It is also important to carry out a review at the end of each day — this could be a part of setting up the next day's programme. Identify those tasks where the allocation of time proved to be realistic, also those where your time planning was less successful. During this process of rationalisation, resolve such questions as 'Am I trying to accomplish too much in a day?' and 'How can I deal more effectively with interruptions?'

Some tasks will require sustained effort over a longer period. In order to monitor progress, a different type of record might be appropriate. The task tracker in figure 12.4 demonstrates one simple, yet effective, format which might be adopted. In the

NO.	THINGS TO DO TODAY	PRIORITY DEADLINE	TIME NEEDED	TARGET ACHIEVED

DAILY PLANNER:

SCHEDULE

9.00

10.00

11.00

12.00

1.00

2.00

3.00

4.00

5.00

EVE.

NOTES :

Figure 12.3 An example of a daily time planner

example given, a Head of Special Needs Support Department was carrying out a consultative process with a view to setting up a whole school policy.

Managing time

It has been said that, if you look in the mirror, you will see your biggest time waster! This seems a harsh comment, but in light of your time audit you may want to consider some strategies which will enhance your use of the time available.

Developing 'helicopter vision'

Helicopter vision was identified by the Shell corporation as being an essential element in the success of its managers. In the same way that a helicopter pilot has a broad view of the landscape, the development of helicopter vision in time management enables a person to take a broader, in-depth view of the job in hand. It is an important pre-requisite in setting clear goals and objectives.

Clear planning

A good operational plan which clearly sets out all of the steps which need to be taken in the process of completing a task will save time. In setting this up, you will need to answer the questions: Why? When? Where? Who? How? and What? Set deadline dates for each stage of the operation and attempt to keep to them. When the plan is aimed at departmental change, active involvement of colleagues in the planning will impart a sense of ownership and ensure that its implementation has a good chance of success.

Dealing with paperwork

One characteristic of educational change is the seemingly obligatory cart load of paper which accompanies it. Class teachers will complete paperwork concerned with the National Curriculum as a matter of necessity. However, a ruthless yet objective approach should be adopted in order to keep the remainder under control.

Firstly, adopt a straightforward filing system and attempt to file important items as you go. This will save considerable time, often wasted in searching for lost documents. Develop an efficient system for dealing with most papers before they reach the filing stage.

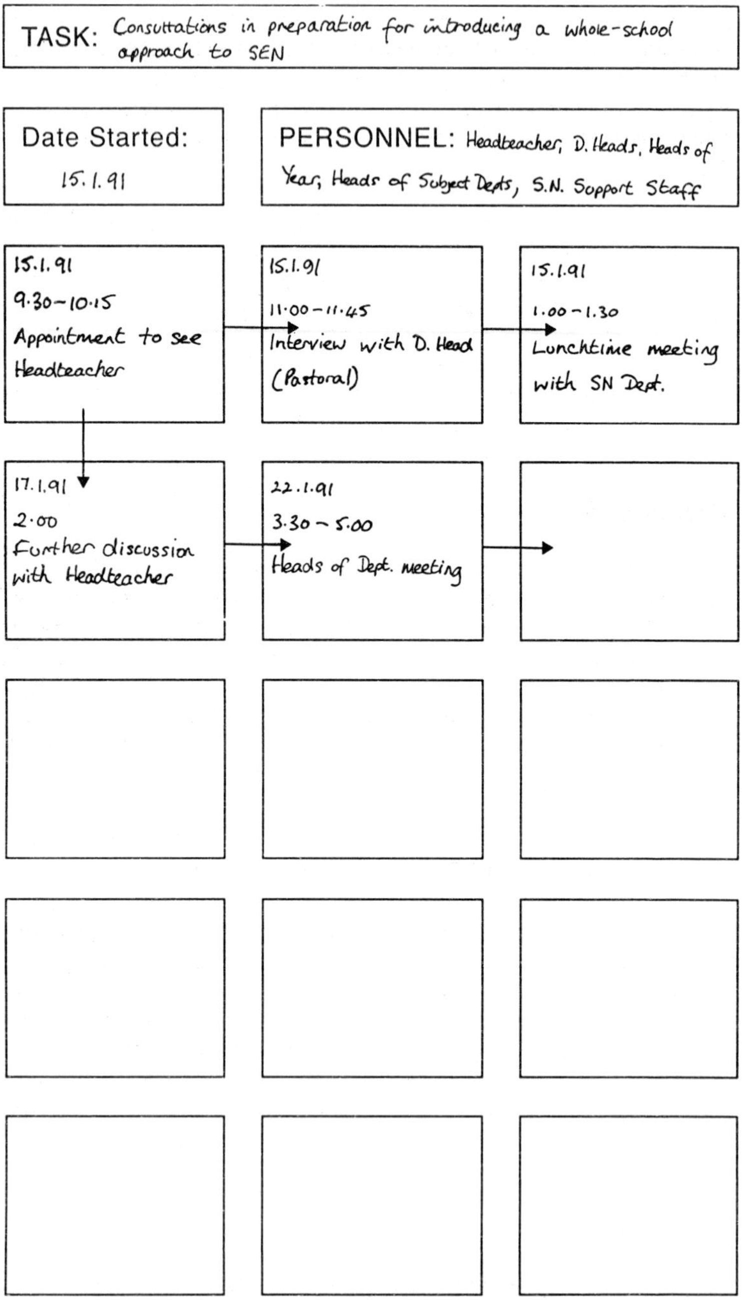

TASK: Consultations in preparation for introducing a whole-school approach to SEN

Date Started:
15.1.91

PERSONNEL: Headteacher, D. Heads, Heads of Year, Heads of Subject Depts, S.N. Support Staff

15.1.91
9.30 – 10.15
Appointment to see Headteacher

15.1.91
11.00 – 11.45
Interview with D. Head (Pastoral)

15.1.91
1.00 – 1.30
Lunchtime meeting with SN Dept.

17.1.91
2.00
Further discussion with Headteacher

22.1.91
3.30 – 5.00
Heads of Dept. meeting

Figure 12.4 Task tracker

Business efficiency experts advocate that your desk should be completely clear, or that you should not leave the building at the end of the day without having first cleared all urgent paperwork. For hard-pressed educationalists this is easier said than done. However, I have used the following system with reasonable success for some years.

1. Position two letter trays on your desk, one on the left-hand side, one on the right.
2. Being left-handed, the tray on the left is for action. In this go all the items for immediate or early attention. I go through this at least once a day and deal with the items.
3. The right-hand tray contains items which need a longer reading time, or which are for information. I go through these when I can, say once a week, reading and filing, as necessary. The remainder is shredded.

Regular reviews

Half-termly or termly reviews of progress, either of a specific project or of the work of the department as a whole, can often be time well spent. Not only does a review meeting bring colleagues together to share views and to discuss queries, but it also provides the opportunity to examine tasks successfully achieved or those objectives which have not yet been fulfilled. The review is also a shared experience in mastering the skills of time management. Planning schedules can be assessed and new deadlines fixed, as necessary.

Getting the best out of meetings

Perhaps it is stating the obvious but, in recent years, the proliferation of meetings seems to have gone hand-in-hand with the pace of educational change. However much we complain about them, meetings are, nevertheless, an important component of our professional lives. It would be difficult to run a school staff, a team or a working group effectively without them. Meetings can be potential time-wasters. This being so, at this point it will be worthwhile reviewing the main reasons for holding meetings. The positive reasons for holding them are:

Communication

A good meeting enables everyone concerned to communicate quickly and accurately. It allows for consultation and negotiation. If relatively large numbers of participants are involved, a meeting can be an efficient use of time and effort.

Creativity

A good meeting draws upon the expertise, knowledge and experience of its participants. It can lead to a flow of ideas which individuals might be less likely to generate on their own.

Decision-making

In recent years, the organisation of education has become much more democratic. A meeting of all those involved can lead to the collective development of an operational plan, the sharing of work, and 'ownership' of a decision. This is more likely to ensure its successful implementation.

Team building

In the process, a good meeting should provide opportunities for individuals to develop empathy towards one another, to cement relationships — it can even be inspiring.

Similarly, we need to remind ourselves of the less valid reasons for calling meetings:

Custom and practice

'We always have a meeting every . . . (Friday, month, half-term etc).' Sticking to routine is hardly a valid reason for holding a meeting. Although the forward planning of diary dates is a part of good time management, there needs to be a sound purpose for convening any meeting, otherwise there is a danger of having a group of committee members in search of an agenda. Beware also of poorly coordinated meetings where participants tend to think out loud, rather than having done their preparation beforehand in order to use the discussion to take matters forward. In the former case, the time allocated is still likely to be filled, even though progress is imperceptible. It is also sometimes apparent that some people tend to avoid their own work by attending or calling a succession of meetings.

Passing the buck

Meetings can sometimes be used as a device to avoid taking difficult decisions. Whilst a trouble shared can be a trouble halved, on some occasions the intention (conscious or unconscious) is to buy time in the hope that someone else will resolve the problem — or that it will disappear altogether.

Democratic fervour

Wide participation in meetings is often healthy, the sharing of responsibilities being a good way of getting the best out of people. However, there are those who are well-intentioned and determined to do the right thing by the democratic process. Frequent meetings are called to share every scrap of information and such an elaborate network of sub-committees and groups is established, that the original purpose of the meeting becomes obscured.

Win or lose situations

Readers will easily identify with some of the situations described. Very often, they will have had little choice in whether or not they should attend such meetings. American business expert, George Kieffer (1988), regards the allocation of time as the most important decision that a person makes in managing his or her professional life. In his view, whenever a person attends a meeting he or she is not only allocating a part of his or her time, but part of life. The decision to attend is either a 'win' or 'lose' situation. He advocates the adoption of a positive attitude:

> Just because you didn't call the meeting, doesn't mean it's not your meeting. Just because you're not chairing the meeting doesn't mean it's not your meeting . . . Your role may vary, your control may be circumscribed, you may have no choice but to attend. Still, if you're there, every meeting is your meeting, too.

Is a meeting necessary?

Poorly planned, unnecessary meetings can lead to the establishment of a negative pattern. After a while your most active participants will be looking for excuses not to attend. Before committing time, pause to consider the alternatives:

— a letter could be sent which outlines a recommended course of action and which asks for any comments or objections;
— a working paper could be circulated, requesting any alterations or amendments;

— you could telephone the persons concerned;
— smaller group meetings could be arranged.

Setting up a successful meeting

There are a number of standard works (such as Locke 1980, Seekings 1981, and Peel 1988) that discuss in detail every aspect of
organising meetings, the roles of participants, group dynamics —
and even meeting 'gamesmanship'. Therefore, the remainder of this
section is confined to considering those aspects likely to have an
influence on the process of change in education.

Kieffer (op cit) concludes that most people spend too little time in
preparation and too much time in meeting. He suggests that more
time spent on the former will not only save time in the long run, but
will also give a stronger likelihood of objectives being achieved.

Define the purpose of the meeting

It is preferable to identify the tasks which need to be undertaken
beforehand and to set a goal for each. A precise statement of what
the meeting has been called to accomplish should be sent to all
concerned. If the main purpose is to make a policy decision, then
careful consideration will need to be given to the information which
has to be circulated beforehand. Alternatively, if the meeting has
been called to develop ideas or to create new ones, a technique such
as *brainstorming* (see Rawlinson 1981) can be effective. This might
not fit into a meeting with a formal agenda.

Drawing up an Agenda

This is more than simply a shopping list of items to be worked
through. A carefully drawn up agenda not only provides the precise
statement previously mentioned, but also sets the tone of the
meeting.

The timing of the introduction of items concerned with change is
crucial to their success. Generally speaking, difficult and contentious items need to be placed early in the agenda, but not right
at the start. They are better faced when the committee has got into
its stride but is still fresh. With regard to items of this nature, be
aware of two traits common to the behaviour of committees. Firstly,
members are more comfortable when they are talking about items
which they know and understand. Since these might be relatively
trivial topics or routine items from previous agendas, they could

occupy time unnecessarily. Secondly, committee members will tend to avoid unfamiliar and complex items, especially those likely to cause mental conflict or those which challenge basic beliefs.

As an example of this, the main committee of a national organisation had an agenda item concerned with members' expenses for travelling to and from meetings. There was an animated discussion as to whether the mileage allowance should be increased to 14p or 16p per mile, during which several members, normally silent, made their views clearly known. The chairperson drew the discussion to an end with some difficulty after 45 minutes. The next agenda item dealt with matters which would shortly lead to a policy decision designed to change the whole structure of the organisation. A report had not been circulated beforehand, therefore a verbal report was made. There were no questions and it was agreed that representatives should proceed with negotiations. The item took seven minutes, at the end of which, the committee moved to its next business.

It is possible that a group meeting for the first time might need to establish an agenda. In this situation, the Nominal Group Technique (Delbecq *et al* 1975) can be helpful. In essence, this allows each participant to make a personal list of items, and then to place these in priority order; these are then pooled with those of other participants, voted on, and a group list of priorities created. This technique can also be used in situations where there is likely to be considerable disagreement about the matters to be discussed. A priority list established in this way not only gives everyone a fair chance but also provides a guideline for future agendas.

Guidelines for becoming a good participant

Bearing in mind Kieffer's dictum that 'every meeting is your meeting too', here are five ways of making positive contributions to meetings:

1. Personal attitude

The essence of a successful meeting is the quality of the interaction between those present. For this to happen, everyone's attitude towards fellow participants should be positive and supportive.

2. Attendance

Unless it is unavoidable, resolve not to attend meetings unless your presence will be justified by your effective contribution.

3. Be prepared

The contributor to a meeting who has prepared carefully beforehand will rarely be caught unawares in discussion. In addition to being well briefed, he or she will be able to anticipate queries and to detect possible 'snares'.

4. Become a good communicator

Active participants at meetings need to be both good listeners and good speakers in order to use both strategies to advantage. Milo (1986) argues that to survive and move ahead in business, or in any other relationship, a person must be able to get his or her point across both succinctly and swiftly. He cites media research which has shown that the attention span of the average person is 30 seconds and that 'if you can't say it in 30 seconds, you probably can't say it at all'. In making a contribution, a person first identifies with his or her listeners and gets to know their expectations. Next, he or she must determine an objective and the line of approach to take. 'When it comes to your 30 second statement, your associates will not only be impressed, they will be grateful.'

5. Be fully conversant with basic procedure

There are a number of procedural rules which are universally accepted for the smooth running of any meeting. Participants ought to:

— obey the chairperson;
— speak only when invited by the chair;
— stick to the point in discussion;
— avoid holding mini-discussions with others during the meeting;
— only interrupt for procedural reasons.

Conversely, there are several leadership functions which are expected of an effective chairperson. He or she should be:

— an attentive listener;
— a clear and rapid thinker;
— able to guide discussion in an impartial manner, also to clarify views;
— able to control the meeting in a firm yet friendly way so that everyone has an equal chance to be heard;

- encouraging participants by making them feel that their contributions are of value to the proceedings;
- able to move business along in a brisk yet sympathetic manner.

Some of the points raised in this short chapter on the management of time and the management of meetings may seem elementary. However, with an increased emphasis on the supportive and consultative elements in special needs work, the question of effective time management has become increasingly significant. Without some form of systematic approach, it is possible for an individual's day to become fragmented with less and less being achieved. The points raised are intended to act as pump-primers in a critical appraisal of current practice.

References and further reading

Adair, J. (1988) *Effective Time Management* London: Pan Books.

Delbecq, A.L., Van de Ven, A.H. and Gustafson, D.H. (1975) *Group Techniques for Programme Planning: a Guide to Nominal Group and Delphi Processes* Glenview, Illinois: Scott Foresman.

Miller, A. and Watts, P. (1990) *Planning and Managing Effective Professional Development* Harlow: Longman.

Kieffer, G.D. (1988) *The Strategy of Meetings* London: Judy Piatkus (Publishers) Ltd.

Locke, M. (1988) *How to Run Committees and Meetings* London: Macmillan.

Milo, F. (1986) *How to Get Your Point Across in 30 Seconds — or Less* London: Corgi Books.

Peel, M. (1988) *How to Make Meetings Work* London: Kogan Page.

Parkinson, C.N. (1957) *Parkinson's Law* Harmondsworth: Penguin.

Rawlinson, J.G. (1981) *Creative Thinking and Brainstorming* Farnborough: Gower.

Seekings, D. (1981) *How to Organise Effective Conferences and Meetings* London: Kogan Page.

13 Behaviour management: a whole-school policy

Colin J. Smith

Teaching has never been a career for anyone who expects their work to be predictable and routine but recent reforms including the National Curriculum, attainment targets, teacher assessment, standard assessment tasks, open enrolment, opting out and teacher appraisal certainly lend weight to the frequently heard assertion that 'it doesn't get any easier does it?' This is particularly true of coping with behaviour problems. Although the horror stories recounted with relish from time to time by the media are not typical and most teachers and children work harmoniously together, where difficulties do exist these are likely to be exacerbated by the new demands being placed upon teachers by recent reforms.

Developing a whole-school policy for coping with behaviour problems involves a combination of four aspects of teaching each beginning with the letter M.

1. Management skills in classroom organisation and lesson presentation.
2. Mediation abilities in providing individual counselling and guidance.
3. Modification programmes for shaping and changing inappropriate behaviour.
4. Monitoring systems which check how school organisation helps to establish and encourage the first three.

Monitoring behaviour policies

In looking at whole-school policy, the emphasis in the present context will be on monitoring. The four Ms should not be seen as a simple linear progression, but as interconnected aspects of a complex process similar in outline to the recommendations made in the advice given by the National Curriculum Council in relation to merging past and future practice for meeting special educational needs (NCC 1989). Four elements which schools need to consider in order to ensure access to the mainstream curriculum are identified:

1. the school's curriculum development plan;
2. its schemes of work;
3. the learning environment;
4. the teaching needs of pupils with learning difficulties and disabilities.

Adapting this approach to formulating a behaviour management policy begins with a *development plan* which identifies priorities and resources for organisational changes. This will provide the starting point described by Stone (1990):

where the school is now, what is working well, what areas need attention and how that attention is to be given.

Collecting and collating information in this way is vital to setting up an effective system for monitoring a behaviour policy.

Whereas the curriculum planning process then moves on to considering schemes of work, the behaviour management plan will take as its next focus a *scheme of discipline* which sets out the structure of responsibilities of different members of staff, particularly with regard to providing support in dealing with serious incidents and emergencies. This scheme will also state official policy on rewards and sanctions and establish a system for recording and evaluating their effectiveness over a specified period of time. This element of the planning process links together aspects of monitoring and modification because it draws attention to whether the school is successful in shaping the behaviour of its pupils.

The equivalent of the learning environment in behaviour management policy concerns the guidance given to teachers on *classroom management*. What are the rules which set the boundaries for acceptable behaviour and what are the routines which regulate the flow of activities within lessons, which the school expects all members of staff to promote? Here the school is monitoring the necessary links between lesson organisation and delivery and the management of group behaviour in classrooms.

Teaching needs in this context become *individual management* and this element concerns the ways in which general policies are aligned with the special needs of pupils whose emotional and behaviour difficulties require additional support. How are such pupils identified and what are the arrangements for counselling them? What steps are taken to make sure that such identification is not merely a means of labelling an inconvenient problem in a manner which defines it as a fault within the child rather than the system? In this instance the school is monitoring its provision for the mediation of individual difficulties.

With its emphasis on these four elements of planning the implementation of the National Curriculum has been helpful in focusing attention and indeed forcing action on whole-school policy and planning. In other ways however recent reforms have not been helpful at all.

Coping with change

Dealing with disruptive pupils will not be helped by the general stress of the effects of an increasingly competitive milieu encouraged by an intention to develop an educational market-place where 'money will follow the pupil'. Senior staff in particular may find more and more of their time taken up with the administration of local management of schools rather than the academic and pastoral care of children. Thinking of children as 'weighted units' used as the currency which buys resources must, in itself, have a depersonalising effect as the language of the factory production line is applied to a much more subtle world traditionally concerned with personal care and nurturing individual growth.

Unless officially designated as pupils whose special needs require the protection of a formal written statement of necessary additional support, disruptive pupils do not attract extra weighting in the formula which allocates funding to schools. This could present a temptation for some schools to regard time spent in dealing with such problems as wasteful of time and effort which might be better spent with more productive 'units'.

Open enrolment is intended to encourage parents to shop around for what they see as the best school for their children and it seems likely that for the most part judgement will be based on examination success or some league table of results measured by the success of pupils in reaching National Curriculum attainment targets. Galloway and Goodwin (1987) have demonstrated there is evidence to show that successful procedures for preventing disturbed behaviour are a 'by-product of processes which aim to raise the overall quality of education for all pupils in the school'. However, it is unlikely that a capacity and willingness to cope with difficult children will rate highly in the criteria used by many parents in selecting schools. Developing behaviour management policies may therefore become associated with finding means for the rapid exclusion of the unusual or abnormal child who threatens the smooth functioning of the academic result production line, rather than finding ways to help the incorporation and improvement of such unpromising raw material within the mainstream of education.

However, it is in coping with the more detailed demands of the National Curriculum for the teaching and assessment of pupils with a wide spread of abilities that more immediate strain will be felt by most teachers, and additional pressure being placed on their skills in classroom organisation and management. The specific behaviour problems which are most frequently encountered in the classroom were identified in the Elton Report (DES 1989). This report was the product of a committee of enquiry into discipline in schools under the chairmanship of Lord Elton. The Committee commissioned special research and took evidence from many expert witnesses about the nature of discipline problems in schools. Its findings confirm a view widely held by teachers that disruptive behaviour in schools is rarely as dramatic or frightening as the occasional individual outrage might suggest. Disruptive behaviour in schools is more a matter of petty annoyances than dangerous aggression.

A national survey of 3500 teachers in 220 primary and 250 secondary schools undertaken for the Elton Committee reflected the findings of an earlier regional survey of 250 Midlands teachers (Houghton, Wheldall and Merrett 1988). These surveys showed that the behaviours which teachers found most frequently troublesome and difficult to deal with were 'talking out of turn', 'hindering other pupils', 'calculated idleness or work avoidance' and 'verbal abuse towards other children'. Thus, it is possible to state with some confidence that minor irritations rather than major confrontations appear to be the main preoccupations in behaviour management in schools.

Examining the demands and likely effects of recent reforms on classroom life suggests that the opportunities for such misbehaviour will be increased by the requirements for group work for the purposes of observation and assessment which are part of the assessment procedures for the National Curriculum. For example, Teacher Assessment as part of normal lesson evaluation and the more formal Standard Assessment Tasks (SATs) will each require a high level of skill in organisation and management in order to keep the rest of the class productively occupied whilst concentrating attention on observing a smaller group which is being assessed.

Most teachers will already have such appropriate skills in classroom management but some teachers, particularly in secondary schools, may not be familiar with working in this way. Early experience with SATs with seven year olds, whose teachers might be expected to be those most used to working with groups on varied tasks, does seem to indicate that even experienced practitioners find it difficult to cope with the additional demands for formal observation and recording whilst, at the same time, keeping normal teaching activities on track. The situation is not helped by the insistence that these assessments should be undertaken single-handed. There is a clear case that such work needs a team rather than an individual approach but, doubtless for financial rather than pedagogic motives, this has been denied. What coping with implementing National Curriculum assessment does show is that it is just as important that school policy should ensure that all teachers receive support and guidance in developing their competence in dealing with such minor irritations, as described above, as it is that school policy should provide a firm system of support for helping teachers respond to more major disciplinary crises.

Reviewing current policy

Comparatively petty problems contribute to what Evans (1981) describes as 'insidious' disruptive behaviour, which if it becomes commonplace, can foster an atmosphere in which more 'excessive' misbehaviours such as defiance and aggression are more likely to occur. Whether or not matters deteriorate to this extent, the acceptance of inappropriate behaviour or failure to deal with it, lowers expectations for teachers and pupils, offers a poor example for good conduct and gives a confused picture of how children should behave. Thus the first stage in developing a whole-school policy for behaviour management is an examination of how effectively the school performs in what have long been defined as the three key features of the 'ethos' of successful schools. These were identified in research by Rutter, Maughan, Mortimore and Ouston (1979) as standards reflecting positive expectations, good models of teacher behaviour exhibiting commitment and concern and effective feedback on what is acceptable conduct. A whole school policy will review and monitor ways in which each of these aspects of school life can be developed and improved.

In order for such a review to be effective, it is important that it should address questions which are sufficiently specific to generate useful information and the opportunity for close scrutiny of actual practice. If questions are too general, it is all too easy for a review to become nothing more than a self-congratulatory exercise in theoretical commitment. What follows is an indication of some of the issues involved in developing and improving each of the three features of the ethos of a successful school.

Positive expectations

Positive expectations are conveyed in a variety of ways both formally and informally, by individual teachers and by institutional practices. As in so many aspects of school life, there is an almost inextricable link between difficulties in learning and behaviour and consequent attitudes towards pupils who display such problems.

> some pupils are low achievers because they lack the motivation to work in school, others because they lack ability. For many both factors are at work.
>
> (DES 1989)

Although this interaction between intellectual and emotional factors has long been acknowledged, there still remains a divide, at least in some secondary schools, between academic and pastoral concerns. A whole-school policy should therefore look for ways of breaking down this artificial divide and integrating a consistently positive approach to academic and personal relationships. Too often the investment of considerable teaching time and energy in trying to build the self-esteem of reluctant learners is unproductive because a contrary message is being delivered by the same pupils being excluded from certain activities or denied access to particular privileges.

Arrangements for exemption, exclusion or disapplication from participation in the National Curriculum are likely to exacerbate such feelings of estrangement from the mainstream. On the other hand, taking the full range of core and foundation subjects may squeeze out of the timetable some of the more imaginative curricular offerings which have been developed in recent years particularly under the aegis of Technical and Vocational Educational Initiatives (TVEI). The apparent lack of relevance of some learning experiences may mean that pupils who see little purpose or point in such activities become disinclined to cooperate.

In this context the issues to be addressed in the process of monitoring school policy concern curriculum planning and the marking and celebration of achievement. How is the curriculum differentiated to meet the needs of less able pupils without this process itself becoming a separatist device? As Montgomery (1990) puts it schools aim for 'differentiation in which all the pupils can share in the same task and gain positively from it'. The National Curriculum is intended to be an 'entitlement' for all children and successful access to it will depend on changes in styles of lesson delivery from teachers and adaptations in the manner of response from pupils.

Developments in examination courses which place an emphasis on coursework and project reports may help maintain pupil involvement and belief in their capacity for achievement and help to avoid or at least reduce disaffection which develops from a sense of inadequacy which follows displacement from the formal system for recognising academic progress. The introduction of individual Records of Achievement and personal profiles, recording the certification of short modules of learning experience and activity, can also help retain the interest and involvement of pupils too easily discarded by traditional systems of evaluation.

The function of the whole-school policy should be to ensure that each subject area and department consistently reviews its own practice in relation to these issues.

Good models

If teachers convey low expectations of their pupils, it is not surprising that some children will live down to them. If teachers themselves offer a poor model of respect for the values which they notionally espouse, it is likely that children will take this as a cue for their own behaviour. As Charlton and David (1989) point out 'modelling' is an important aspect of learning sets of behaviours. If teachers turn up late and unprepared for lessons, don't mark and return work promptly and let anger rapidly escalate to punitive or even physical intervention, then they should not be surprised when pupils show a similar lack of concern for punctuality and reliability and an equally abrasive response to irritation.

It can be argued that, as far as behaviour is concerned, children learn as much, if not more, from how teachers themselves behave than they do from what they say. Schools in which teachers are made aware of this perspective will encourage staff to display good models of behaviour by demonstrating in their classrooms the repertoire of conduct recommended by Charlton and David (1989) which includes:

1. showing respect for pupils by listening to them with interest and refraining from harsh or sarcastic criticism of their views;
2. showing sensitivity to fears, anxieties and inadequacies and being ready and willing to help overcome them;

3. controlling their own emotions and acknowledging responsibility for personal errors;
4. responding appropriately to justifiable criticism of their own actions.

Fontana (1986) discusses teacher qualities in terms of aspects of temperament and personality to which pupils respond favourably. These commendable attributes include: fairness in providing equal opportunities and equal attention; humour and the ability to laugh *with* not *at* the class; calmness and a relaxed manner which remains unruffled when problems do arise; patience in the face of frustration, and the ability to explain things clearly at an appropriate cognitive level.

Teachers will differ in their ability and inclination to demonstrate good models of behaviour, but a whole-school policy should provide guidelines about how teachers are expected to behave and offer opportunities for discussion and advice about how these guidelines can be applied in practice. Gray and Richer (1988) indicate some useful topics for such discussion noting that pupil insecurity arising from frustration is the prime source of disruptive behaviour.

1. How do teachers strike a balance between work and social contact in the classroom?
2. How do teachers recognise each pupil's starting point in a particular subject so that expectations are appropriate?
3. How can rules be minimised and rationalised so that behaviour is adequately regulated without frequent injunctions?
4. How can commands be phrased as requests to reduce the likelihood of confrontation?
5. How can teachers express pleasantness and humanity towards their pupils, showing personal interest and liking without losing authority?

The function of the whole-school policy should be to see that staff do meet to review and discuss these issues and reach a consensus sufficient to establish a predictable pattern of teacher behaviour.

Effective feedback

Other aspects of the planning process described above will define what is a school's perception of acceptable conduct but attention also has to be given to how pupils are made aware of whether they are behaving in ways which satisfy this perception. Essentially, this feature concerns analysing classroom organisation and getting teachers to reflect on the effectiveness of their communication with pupils. Smith (1990) suggests various areas of organisation which can be used as a framework for such reflection. The following are particularly relevant to providing clear and effective feedback:

1. Rules and routines

How are these established so that pupils will accept that they are rational and sensible? Do they help reduce the potential misinterpretation and enable pupils to anticipate events? As Lovitt (1977) memorably put if 'if children know what we want they will usually do it'.

2. Assignments and rewards

Are tasks differentiated and matched to pupil ability so that there is a reasonable prospect for successful achievement for each individual? Is marking frequent, informative and constructive? Do all pupils feel that they can share in whatever reward system is in operation?

3. Individual recognition

Are pupils known and recognised as individuals by teachers? Are teaching styles varied through group work so that the visibility and personality of individuals become more evident than in the whole-class-lecture situation? What help is given to teachers in developing more varied approaches and do classroom layout and design foster or frustrate such initiatives?

4. Providing support

How are tasks allocated so that time is available for individual attention? What help is available through suitably prepared study guides or topic outlines to encourage self-guided learning? Are teachers trained in developing supplementary material to occupy pupil waiting time? Is there support from specialist teachers for meeting the needs of pupils with difficulties in learning?

This last question neatly returns consideration to the likely effects of recent reforms. Over the last decade the concept of support teaching has gained acceptance. Whilst the option of withdrawal from certain lessons for intensive individual or small group teaching may still be appropriate in some circumstances, there has been growing acceptance that team teaching is the best approach to meeting special needs. This has involved specialist staff helping colleagues by working alongside them, sharing skills and expertise so that all teachers develop confidence in adapting methods and materials to match curricular demands to a diversity of individual differences in levels of ability.

Whether such assistance is from specialist staff within schools or from peripatetic learning support services, it does seem likely that one effect of the introduction of local management of schools may be to constrain the funding available to provide support for pupils with special educational needs as part of a team-teaching approach. Schools will be faced with difficult decisions about allocation of limited resources within their staffing structure or the expenditure of limited funds on buying in outside help. There will be a strong incentive to limit any such spending to those pupils who have been officially 'statemented'. Whether intended or not it appears that support teaching, developed with local and national approval during the last decade may not prosper in the next. In this respect, as in many others noted above, whilst coping with change may present valuable opportunities to appraise and amend current practice in behaviour management, it is difficult not to concur with those teachers who claim that 'it doesn't get any easier, does it?'

References

Charlton, T. and David, K. (eds.) (1989) *Managing Misbehaviour: Strategies for Effective Management of Behaviour in Schools* Basingstoke: Macmillan.

DES (1989) *Discipline in Schools* The Elton Report London: HMSO.

Evans, M. (1981) *Disruptive Pupils* London: Schools Council.

Fontana, D. (1986) *Classroom Control: Understanding and Guiding Classroom Behaviour* London: Methuen.

Galloway, D. and Goodwin, C. (1987) *The Education of Disturbing Children* London: Longman.

Gray, J. and Richer, J. (1988) *Classroom Responses to Disruptive Behaviour* Basingstoke: Macmillan.

Houghton, S. and Wheldall, K. and Merrett, F. (1988) Classroom behaviour problems which secondary school teachers say they find most troublesome British *Education Research Journal*, **14**, 3.

Lovitt, T.C. (1977) *In Spite of My Resistance I've Learned from Children* Columbus, Ohio: Merrill.

Montgomery, D. (1990) *Children with Learning Difficulties* London: Cassell.

NCC (1989) *A Curriculum for All: Special Educational Needs in the National Curriculum* National Curriculum Council, Curriculum Guidance 2, London.

Rutter, M., Maughan, B., Mortimore, P. and Ouston, J. (1979) *Fifteen Thousand Hours* London: Open Books.

Smith, C.J. (1990) 'Analysing classroom organisation' in Scherer, M. Gersch, I. and Fry, L. (eds.) *Meeting Disruptive Behaviour: Assessment, Intervention and Partnership* Basingstoke: Macmillan.

Stone, L. (1990) *Managing Difficult Children in School* Oxford: Basil Blackwell.

14 Classroom organisation to meet special needs

Gary Thomas

The question of classroom organisation and management is a difficult one to write about. As all experienced teachers know (but as politicians seem incapable of understanding) it cannot be answered with recipes for successful practice. An element of art enters into the interpretation of all recipes, as anyone who tastes my pastry will attest. I do try to follow the recipe, in fact I follow it religiously, but it never quite works out. There is, I have discovered, more to making pastry than simply following the recipe. Classroom management is no different. It is a complex blend of art and science — of skills and knowledge which have been learned from a teacher or a book, and skills which have been learned on the job.

I shall try to avoid the trap of suggesting that recipes play any part in an understanding of classroom management for special needs. What I hope that this chapter will provide is a framework which will help to organise experience. I shall structure this framework via a number of questions, grouped under, 1 context and 2 organisation. Thus:

1. Context
   — Why teach in an integrated way?
   — Which children should be taught?
   — What should be taught?

2. Organisation
— When will teaching take place?
— Where will teaching happen?
— Who will do the teaching?
— How will they do the teaching?

The main point which I wish to address in this chapter is that some learning needs (and thus some special needs) can be met simply by changing the organisation of the classroom. Such an apparently simple suggestion unfortunately competes poorly with the pseudo-scientific suggestions which have often come out of special needs education. Often we have sought all kinds of arcane reasons for children's difficulties in class and we have come up with mysterious-sounding syndromes to explain away these difficulties. *Auditory sequencing* or *visuo-motor processing* sounds technical enough to impress anyone that we have worked out a child's difficulties and are in a position to work effectively on solving those difficulties. Unfortunately, though, the evidence is that such diagnoses (based on a *deficit approach* or the assumption that the child has something wrong with him or her) are ineffective in actually helping children. Remedial programmes based on such diagnoses are no more effective than programmes based on teachers' unguided judgements (see Johnson and Pearson 1975, Newcomer and Hammill 1987).

It is probably true to say that special needs educators have spent too much time devising special methods of assessment and teaching. Even if these had been shown to work (which they haven't) there would be the problem of working out how to use these time-consuming methods in the integrated classroom, where there are the needs of the other 30 children also to consider.

Given the ethos about which I have spoken already, it is far more appropriate that special needs are met through changes in organisation rather than through changes in teaching method.

Let us return, then, to the questions outlined above.

The context

The first set of questions outlined earlier, the contextual questions, are not as centrally related to the issue of classroom organisation as the last four but a discussion of them is essential before proceeding to discuss the latter. They provide the context and the rationale for the more nitty gritty questions of classroom management.

Why teach in an integrated way?

During the 1960s and 1970s there were increasing calls for the integration of disabled people into society. People who had received a segregated education 'for their own good' resented the limitations which this had put on their educational opportunities; they resented the stigma which had been imposed upon them; they resented a system which enabled the majority to grow up thinking that the minority simply did not exist.

At the same time, research into the effectiveness of special education was emerging. It showed quite consistently that such education was not as effective as we would expect it to be, given the very much greater amounts of money per child being spent on it. It indicated that children who were educated in mainstream schools did as well, or better than, comparable children who had been through special education (see Galloway and Goodwin 1979 for a discussion).

The Warnock Committee (DES 1978) was set up to re-evaluate special educational provision in the light of this changing climate. It suggested that categories of handicap be abolished and be replaced with the more general notion of special educational need; it was broadly in favour of integration. The 1981 Education Act was the legislative framework, albeit somewhat toothless, which implemented the committee's recommendations.

Which children should be taught?

It is within this framework that integration is happening (though not as fast as many would like). Alongside it is the notion that a larger body of children, one in five according to Warnock, should be assumed to have special educational needs. These are the children who are already in mainstream schools but who are experiencing difficulties. It is both these children and the much smaller minority who will be integrating from special schools whom we must think about when considering the question of classroom management.

If the principle of integration is correct, as surely it must be, how can it be made to work effectively? It requires more than simply teaching children with special needs in the ordinary school. It requires that those children should be taught *in the same classes* as their peers. To remove them to a withdrawal setting is only another form of segregation.

Another important notion as far as the Warnock recommendations and the 1981 Act were concerned was the concept of special need replacing the idea of categories of handicap. Children's needs could not be described simply by attaching a label to them. There came to be a recognition that to say that a child had *learning difficulties* or *Down's Syndrome* or *cerebral palsy* did nothing to describe what the child actually needed in order to make progress. There came to be a recognition that children might experience difficulties at any time in their school careers; that special needs did not reside in a fixed, unchanging group of children, rather, special needs might exist briefly or for long periods, depending on both the children and the nature of the learning being undertaken.

The new notion of special needs, then, demands that we approach the question of which children we teach in a much more flexible way than has ever been the case. It is not so much a question now of identifying, perhaps through tests, a group of children who will be in need of help. Rather, the onus is now on mainstream and support personnel to identify and deal with learning problems as and when they arise.

What should be taught?

Simply to have certain children remain in the ordinary class, only to be taught or helped in that setting by specialist personnel, takes us no further toward a true realisation of the ideal of integration. To have a certain group of children in receipt of special teaching in the mainstream class is simply another form of segregation, only in this case more visibly than previously. In order for these children to be truly integrated they will need to be in mixed ability settings, participating in the same activities as the other children in the class.

Over the years, the area of special educational needs has produced a range of methods of helping children, and these have usually involved a change in the curriculum. Not only this, but they have also involved changes in methods of assessment or teaching. The problem now, and increasingly, is that in the integrated settings in which those methods have to be delivered, there are a host of factors which will conspire against their success. Mainstream teachers, who will bear the main responsibility for meeting special needs, will find it difficult or impossible to find the time for mastering or using these special methods if they are not to neglect their responsibilities to the main body of the children in the class. Neither, it must be said, are these different methods, which special educators have been so good at promulgating, renowned for their success (see, for example, Cashdan *et al.* 1971, Hargreaves 1978, Thomas 1985a, Algozzine, Morsink and Algozinne 1986).

The National Curriculum has in many ways resolved questions over whether some children should be receiving a different curriculum from others. It makes it clear that *all* children should study the same curriculum, the National Curriculum, whether they be in special schools or ordinary schools (unless the headteacher of a mainstream school feels the need to 'disapply' the National Curriculum to individuals for limited periods of time).

So, now it is clear; the Education Reform Act removes the

ambiguities. All children are entitled to the National Curriculum. It is no longer sufficient to exempt certain pupils from large sections of the curriculum to receive special remedial help. To effect this requirement of the legislation surely demands that we seek ways of making mixed ability teaching work.

If it is inappropriate that changes in curriculum or teaching method should be sought in order to make mixed ability teaching work, then the logical conclusion is that the learning environment be made more congenial, via changes in the organisation of the class.

The organisation

Following a discussion of the context within which organisation for special needs has to be thought about, what are the implications?

This requires questions to be answered not simply about meeting special needs, but questions about meeting learning needs generally. One of the implications of the previous section is that *categories* do not describe *need*. *Need* can only be described in terms of an outcome. If children are to make progress, they have a number of possible needs. They need to be interested; they need help; they may need to be able to discuss; they may need peace and quiet to be able to think things through. These are the needs children have in order to be able to learn and to make progress. Special needs are no different, though we must be a little more vigilant about ensuring that these needs are met when children are conspicuously experiencing difficulties.

If needs are conceptualised in this way, and if we are expecting that all children receive substantially the same curriculum in a mixed ability setting, then it is only a short step to saying that needs may most effectively be met through:

1. examining what comprises *learning needs*;
2. examining how we can meet those *needs* through changes in *classroom organisation*.

It was suggested above that in order to learn you need:

— to be interested;
— to be motivated;
— to be concentrating;
— help from others;
— to be confident.

It was further suggested that special needs are no different from these ordinary needs. More sensitivity to these learning needs is necessary with some children, but in general the laws of learning are the same whoever you are. If this is the case, then learning needs can be met through changing the organisation of the classroom. Examination of the ways in which this may be possible can take place by asking *when* learning is to occur, *where* it is to occur, *who* will give the help and *how* that help is to be organised.

When will teaching take place?

One of the central findings to come out of half a century of behavioural psychology is this: *you get better at the things that you practise.* (Millions of dollars in hundreds of research grants have been spent proving this.) The more practice you have, the better you get. With any given task or skill there will, of course, be variations in the amount of practice needed to achieve a certain level of competence in the task. Some people will take more time and some less. But the principle stays the same: progress comes through practice. Therefore, *a classroom should provide regular opportunities for undertaking new tasks and activities.*

Another finding which has been made is that, in general, if people are presented with new skills to be learned or new ideas to be understood they learn best if learning takes place in frequent short doses. Ten six-minute sessions are likely to be more fruitful than one 60 minute session. (Psychologists call the former *distributed* practice and the latter *massed* practice.) This is particularly so if children have experienced difficulties. If they are in the 'set' of failing, they will tend to lose concentration very quickly. It is particularly important that in a situation such as this, children aren't allowed to become bored and frustrated by having too much asked of them. Again, the principle is the same for everyone: *distributed practice is better than massed practice.*

These, then, are important learning needs. They may be addressed through thinking about the ways in which additional people in the classroom organise their work (see '*How* will they do the teaching', below).

Where will teaching happen?

One of the points which have been made in this chapter is the *need* for absence from distraction in order to make progress with some activities. To do some tasks a little peace and quiet is required. Some children seem to become distracted more easily than others, so for them the need for absence from distraction is particularly important. There is immediate room here for thinking about the ways in which the physical organisation of the classroom may in itself meet special needs.

Most classrooms are organised into groups. The reasons for this lie in the Plowden principles of allowing children to cooperate and communicate. Those principles and that ethos are as important now as ever, and there is certainly still a very strong argument for continuing these ideals.

However, when examination takes place of what is actually happening in classrooms, we find that children are not predominantly doing group work in these groups: they are doing individual tasks instead (see Galton, Simon and Croll 1980). Now, the very features of groups which make them good for doing group work (the ability to make eye contact, the ability to talk easily to the person opposite) make them not so good for doing the kind of individual tasks that are actually being asked of them in class.

Before going any further, I must make it clear that I am not advocating an abandonment of group work. The point is simply that groups are an organisational format which is particularly suited to group work. Other organisational formats are more suited to other kinds of activity. It is for the teacher to decide the activity he or she is asking of the children. If he or she is asking the children to undertake individual work, it seems less than appropriate to sit the children in an arrangement which hinders the effective undertaking of that activity.

How, then, can classroom organisation — classroom geography if you like — be changed to help meet the children's learning needs?

Weinstein (1979) in a major review of classroom research cites some interesting studies which suggest possible answers to this question. One particularly interesting case study compares two classrooms which are similar in all but classroom geography. In classroom A, desks were arranged so that only two or three children could work together; areas for different activities were set apart by barriers such as bookcases, and areas for quiet study and areas for activities were also set apart; the teacher's desk was in the corner so that she was unable to direct activities from it and had to move around the room a great deal. Here, conversation was quieter, and the children were more engaged, with longer attention spans than those in classroom B.

Classroom B was less appropriately organised. In classroom B large groups of children (up to 12) were supposed to be working together (despite the individualised curriculum); areas for different activities were not clearly designated and the teacher's desk was centrally located — enabling her to direct activity from her seat.

The implication from this kind of study is that certain forms of organisation can actually encourage — or hinder — certain kinds of activity in both the children and the teacher. They can encourage or hinder concentration. They can encourage or hinder the engagement of the children.

There is other evidence about the importance of the physical organisation of the classroom. For instance, children appear to prefer non-traditionally organised classrooms (i.e. not organised in the traditional Plowden format with groups). Pfluger and Zola (1974), for instance, found that children preferred a large space in the centre of the room, with furniture along the walls. Children may even prefer being in formal rows rather than being in groups (see Bennett and Blundell 1983, Wheldall *et al.* 1981).

Important also for the organisation of the classroom where meeting special needs is concerned is the evidence (Delefes and Jackson 1972) that an 'action zone' exists in many classrooms; most of the teacher's interactions occur with children at the front and in the middle of the class (this is even in classrooms which in theory have no front). Research shows (Saur *et al.* 1984) that if an action zone exists, then hearing-impaired children who happen to be sitting at the periphery of the class are doubly disadvantaged. Not only children with sensory disabilities will be handicapped by the action zone: withdrawn children, or the 'intermittent workers' of the ORACLE study (Galton *et al.* 1980) might also be doubly disadvantaged by the existence of such a zone. There is clearly scope here for thinking about the geography of the classroom, the movement of the teacher around the classroom and the placement of certain children within the class if those children's needs are to be met appropriately.

Lucas and Thomas (1990) have shown how the reorganisation of the typical Plowden classroom may go a long way toward meeting learning needs — and therefore special learning needs.

Who will do the teaching?

Wherever teaching is taking place and however carefully it is planned, there is a crucial question which comes into the reckoning in determining how it is undertaken. This concerns the effective integration not simply of the *children* but, perhaps more problematically, of the *adults* who are associated with them. If integration is to operate effectively, a very wide range of people will be expected to work alongside the class teacher in the mainstream classroom. They will be required to form new kinds of classroom teams. However, very little thought has been given to the question of how these people will work together as teams.

It may be worth briefly enumerating the kinds of personnel who will comprise these new teams.

1. Peripatetic teachers are beginning to provide help for children and for mainstream teachers by working alongside the class teacher in the classroom. This takes the place of the practice of withdrawing children, a practice which may stigmatise the children who are withdrawn.
2. It is becoming increasingly common to find that local authorities are seeking to make special arrangements for children with special needs in ordinary schools rather than placing them in special schools; in practice, these arrangements often include the allocation of a welfare assistant to work with a child in his/her classroom for a set period of time in a week.
3. In secondary and middle schools there has been a change from systems of withdrawal to a range of new team-teaching arrangements. In these new arrangements, those teachers who would at one time have been called remedial teachers now work alongside mainstream colleagues. They are now often designated *support* teachers.
4. In some local authorities, 'outreach' schemes are enabling the devolution of the skills of special school teachers (who remain on the special school staff) to mainstream classrooms.

The success of integration hinges on the effective assimilation into mainstream education of these 'special' personnel and resources; in some cases it may be possible to meet special needs through the provision of equipment or through adaptation of the physical environment. By contrast, the assimilation of human resources from special settings is infinitely more complex and more problematic.

Unfortunately, the record of teamwork in classrooms (see Geen 1985, Cohen 1976) does not augur well for these new teams. Transferring people from the special to the mainstream setting will not be a smooth, seamless transition. Expertise and skills will not be transposed effortlessly.

All kinds of difficulties will afflict these new teams. They may be marked by interpersonal clashes, ideological differences, problems of role definition (who is supposed to be doing what?), and simple practical problems over, for instance, finding time to discuss appropriate ways of working. Given these difficulties I have suggested elsewhere (Thomas 1991) that the new classroom teams operate within the following organisational parameters:

1. The shared classroom should be seen in the context of developments which are worthwhile and worthy of promotion by the school. The formulation of a whole-school policy on educational needs will be beneficial, if the whole staff,

including all support personnel, is genuinely involved in the process of developing such policy.

2. Opportunity should exist from the outset in the new teams for discussion about the pedagogic, professional and affective concerns and expectations of team members. Tension which arises out of mismatch between participants' concerns and expectations appears to be at the root of team defences which inhibit teams' effective working.

3. However, mismatches in the team should not assume an unwarranted significance. Teamwork stresses are likely to be handled more successfully through clear task and role definition than through strenuous attempts to resolve mismatches through improved communication among participants. Strategies directing attention to the *task* are more likely to meet with success than those directing attention to the *participants*.

4. Planning for teaming will ideally be a joint exercise involving all classroom participants. People need to be able to discuss the roles they will be fulfilling and whether they would feel comfortable undertaking a particular set of tasks. The opportunity of exchanging and interchanging roles needs to be discussed.

5. Individuals' strengths and weaknesses need to be identified during planning.

6. Clear definition of classroom tasks and activities needs to be made during planning.

7. The composition of the team needs to be considered carefully. There are grounds for believing that heterogeneous teams (e.g. teams comprising teacher and welfare assistant) will experience fewer stresses than homogeneous teams (e.g. teams comprising two teachers).

8. The team needs to meet regularly to discuss and evaluate the way that they have been working. The openness of a 'quality circle' has to be the hallmark of such meetings; the atmosphere should be informal with individuals encouraged to suggest ideas.

The key elements of these recommendations — about communication, acceptance of the ideas of others, willingness to make changes — may seem too obvious to state. But it is all too clear that unless these points are explicitly made they are often ignored: the obvious eludes us and commonsense flies out of the window when we work under the weight of an organisational culture.

Indeed, that culture often actively ignores the possible problems of the new teams. It assumes (wishful thinking, perhaps) that there are no negative consequences associated with these new moves. It therefore allocates no time for the new team members to discuss the ways in which they will work together. The result is that team members are forced to squeeze the crucial processes of planning, review and evaluation into the few moments before or after a lesson. Given the possible problems of the new teams, this is hopelessly inadequate.

How will they do the teaching?

Given the context outlined at the outset of this chapter, certain principles should guide the operation of the people who work together in the new classroom teams.

1. There should be an assumption that special needs may arise anywhere and at any time in the class. Special needs do not reside within a pre-specified group of children. Therefore, special personnel will be aiming to work more flexibly than they have previously done, identifying needs as and when they occur, rather than identifying a particular group of children and working exclusively with those.

2. If one of the needs which some children have is the need for more individual help, then there is room for thinking about specialisation in the roles which the new teamworkers undertake. Given the ambiguities which exist when the new support teams are formed, such a specification of role will in itself be of value by reducing this ambiguity. The central purpose of such specialisation, however, will be in enabling the provision of additional help to those who need it while, at the same time, catering for the wider needs of the whole class. A programme such as 'room management' (see Thomas 1985b) may be of value in helping to determine the precise nature of these roles.

Conclusion

Changing the organisation of the classroom is an unusual way of meeting needs, yet it is far more in tune with post-Warnock thinking than more traditional methods. It does not necessarily involve the identification of individual children, nor does it involve the construction and execution of complex teaching or remedial programmes.

By matching organisation with teaching aims it may be possible to stop certain difficulties arising, and it may be possible to help children who are experiencing difficulties. Significant changes can be made in the way the classroom is organised to cater for special needs, and indeed for the learning needs of all the children in the class.

References

Algozzine, K.M., Morsink, C.V. and Algozzine, B. (1986) 'Classroom ecology in categorical special education classrooms' *Journal of Special Education* **20**, 2, 209–217.

Bennett, N. and Blundell, D. (1983) 'Quantity and quality of work in rows and classroom groups' *Educational Psychology* **3**, 2, 93–105.

Cashdan, A., Pumfrey, P.D. and Lunzer, E.A. (1971) 'Children receiving remedial treatment in reading' *Educational Research* **13**, 2, 98–103.

Delefes, P. and Jackson, B. (1972) 'Teacher pupil interaction as a function of location in the classroom' *Psychology in the Schools* **9**, 119–123.

Cohen, E.G. (1976) 'Problems and prospects of teaming' *Educational Research Quarterly* **1**, 2, 49–63.

Department of Education and Science (1978) *Special Educational Needs* Report of the Committee of Enquiry into the Education of Handicapped Children and Young People, Cmnd 7212, London: HMSO.

Galloway, D.M. and Goodwin, C. (1979) *Educating Slow Learning and Maladjusted Children: Integration or Segregation?* Harlow: Longman.

Galton, M.J., Simon, B. and Croll, P. (1980) *Inside the Primary Classroom* London: Routledge and Kegan Paul.

Green, A.G. (1985) 'Team teaching in the secondary schools of England and Wales' *Educational Review* **37**, 1, 29–38.

Hargreaves, D.H. (1978) 'The proper study of educational psychology' *Association of Educational Psychologists' Journal* **4**, 9, 3–8.

Johnson, D.D. and Pearson, P.D. (1975) 'Skills management systems: a critique' *Reading Teacher* **28** 757–765.

Lucas, D. and Thomas, G. (1990) 'The geography of classroom learning' *British Journal of Special Education* **17**, 1, 31–34.

Newcomer, P.L. and Hammill, D.D. (1975) 'ITPA and academic achievement' *Reading Teacher* **28**, 731–742.

Pfluger, L.W. and Zola, J.M. (1974) 'A room planned by children' in Coates, G.J. (ed.) *Alternative Learning Environments*. Stroudsberg, Pa: Dowden, Hutchinson and Ross.

Saur, R.E., Popp, M.J. and Isaacs, M. (1984) 'Action zone theory and the hearing impaired student in the mainstreamed classroom' *Journal of Classroom Interaction* **19**, 2, 21–25.

Thomas, G. (1985a) 'What psychology had to offer education — then' *Bulletin of the British Psychological Society* **38**, 322–326.

Thomas, G. (1985b) 'Room management in mainstream education' *Educational Research* **27**, 3, 186–194.

Thomas, G. (1991) The new classroom teams: their nature, dynamics and difficulties. Unpublished doctoral thesis, Oxford Polytechnic.

Weinstein, C.S. (1979) 'The physical environment of the school: a review of the research' *Review of Educational Research* **49**, 4, 577–610.

Wheldall, K., Morris, M., Vaughan, P. and Ng, Y.Y. (1981) 'Rows v. tables: an example of the use of behavioural ecology in two classes of eleven-year-old children' *Educational Psychology* **1**, 2, 171–184.

Part V
Liaison

15 Working with governors to meet special educational needs

Graham Bill

There must be many who, as teachers, have applied for positions in schools and have been subjected to 'interview by governor'. At an interview in Wolverhampton in 1981 the candidates were assembled in the deputy headteacher's office. The headteacher walked in looking a little sheepish. 'I am sorry,' he said, 'but at the last governors' meeting I invited any governor interested to sit on the interview panel. I am afraid eight of them have turned up. So that means with the senior adviser, myself, the chairman of the governors and my deputy there are twelve people doing the interviewing.' Fortunately most of them kept quiet and remained as observers on the back row except a newly appointed parent governor who asked what was the candidates' opinion concerning the compulsory wearing of school uniform. There was no appointment made that day. I would imagine that it was difficult to come to some consensus of opinion amongst such a large group. But that interview heralded the beginning of the new age in school management. It was the birth of the active governor.

Prior to the 1980 Education Act governors had been regarded by teachers as a group of rather distant figures many of whom were never seen by the staff other than when they sat on the stage at prize giving. They were regarded very much as the butcher, the baker and the candlestick-maker type of persons who had managed to gain some kudos by becoming a school governor and who knew very little about actual school affairs. They would sit at governors' meetings and receive reports from the headteacher and leave any active involvement to the chairman who usually had some tenuous link with education.

In the first paragraph of the Education Act of 1980 the tone was set for the rest of the Acts in the 1980s:

> . . . shall be known as governors instead of managers and the instrument providing for the constitution of that body as an instrument of government instead of management.
>
> (1.1)

This first educational pronouncement of the 1980s may have seemed of little importance at that time but, in retrospect, the political connotation of the word 'governor' as opposed to 'manager' was deeply significant. Also, the compulsory inclusion of both parent and teacher governors heralded the trend to more involved and effective government of schools and paved the way for the Education Act of 1986.

However, there had been a suggestion made earlier by the Warnock Report (DES 1978) that also had a significant effect on the 'special needs' thinking that went into both the 1986 and 1988 Education Acts. Having highlighted the importance of the governing body being made aware of the significant proportion of children with special educational needs in an ordinary school at any one time, also the importance of the governing body being made aware of any special classes or units set up within the school, the report goes on to say:

> '. . . we recommend that where a special class or unit established by a local education authority is attached to an ordinary school, a member of the managing or governing body should be specifically concerned with that class or unit.

This seed of the *named governor* that was sown so early was to take nearly ten years to germinate but, when it did, it was to take on a much wider role than simply special classes and units within an ordinary school.

Governors' responsibilities

The Education Act 1981, which followed the Warnock Report, makes some general points which apply to governors' responsibilities to children with special educational needs in mainstream schools. Section 2.5 states that they must 'use their best endeavours' to ensure that appropriate provision is made for each individual and to ensure that teachers of children with special educational needs are informed as to the nature of each pupil's need. They must also endeavour to see that teachers are aware of the importance of identification and provision for pupils with special educational needs.

In section 2.7 responsibility is put on all concerned with the making of provision for SEN to ensure, where a pupil with special educational needs is educated in an ordinary school, that he or she 'engages in the activities of the school together with children who do not have special needs'. There are, however, provisos attached to this requirement and they are:

1.   that the pupil receives the special education provision that he or she requires;
2.   that an efficient education is provided for the other pupils;
3.   that there is efficient use of resources;
4.   that the functional integration is 'reasonably practicable'.

These conditions have caused much discussion in many governors' meetings.

The Education (No 2) Act 1986 should be seen as the foundation for the Education Reform Act 1988. Important changes to the composition and powers of governing bodies were made in the 1986 Education Act, then the Education Reform Act 1988 increased the powers of the governing body considerably. Far more responsibility for the financial running of the school was given to the governors. This included the responsibility for informing parents and the local community about the performance of the school in relation to the curriculum, staffing, admissions policy and discipline.

Whilst the power of the governing body was increased, so was the representation of parents. Between one quarter to one third of governing bodies can now be made up of parents. By those teachers who have been involved with teaching children with special educational needs this can be seen as a mixed blessing. The special needs teachers has always encouraged parental involvement. There have been many schemes to encourage parents into the school — 'paired reading' in primary schools springs to mind, also the involvement of parents in extra-curricular activities in both primary and secondary schools. Special needs teachers are fighting a constant battle to encourage parents, who themselves have had unfortunate experiences at school, to become involved with their children's education. To have parents in such a powerful driving position would seem the ideal thing but, as so often happens, the involvement of the parent of the child with special needs is the exception rather than the rule. One head of an SEN department, a teacher governor of long standing, has already said that parent governors who had previously supported her policy for admission of pupils with specific learning difficulties are now actively discouraging the admission of these pupils as they tend to be expensive on resources and are of little value when the school has to be marketed.

Duties towards pupils with special needs

A side effect of this shift of power has been felt mostly in primary schools where, prior to the Education Reform Act, the provision of extra help to meet the special educational needs of pupils had rested with the advisory and support services. Now, with the delegation of budgets under the Local Management of Schools (LMS), governors are finding themselves responsible for allocating part of the school's financial resource to this area. Here is the dilemma. If, as a parent governor, your child misses out on some aspect of school life because the headteachers wants to increase teacher provision for special educational needs, how do you vote? For far less money you can employ unqualified classroom assistance which may well satisfy the law. This brings us to the duty of governors towards the pupils with special educational needs and it is important that all teachers are aware of them.

What are the governors' duties to pupils with special education needs?

Governors should ensure as far as possible that any special provision required by a pupil in school is made. They should also:

> secure that, where the responsible person has been informed by the local education authority that a registered pupil has special educational needs, those needs are made known to all who are likely to teach him.
>
> Education Act 1981 (2.5b)

The responsible person would usually be the headteacher but it could be the Chairman of the Governors or a governor appointed by the governing body to take responsibility. Governors should also:

> secure that teachers in the school are aware of the importance of identifying, and providing for, those registered pupils who have special educational needs.
>
> Education Act 1981 (2.5c)

Governors should ensure that:

> Where a child who has special education needs . . . so far as is . . .
> reasonably practicable, that the child engages in the activities of
> the school together with the children who do not have special
> educational needs.
>
> Education Act 1981 (2.7)

Governors should also ensure that the parents are involved at an
early stage and their views are taken into account in making
provision for a child's special educational needs.

There are five distinct areas here in which governors have
responsibility under the law. These areas can be classified as
provision, dissemination, awareness, access and *parents*. If they are
going to comply with the requirements that ensure these areas are
covered in each school then the teaching staff must cooperate wholly
with the governors to see that they are well informed about the structure for special needs within the school, the size of the problem
being tackled by the staff and the availability of resources both
within and from without the school both material and human. The
governors must also be aware of processes of assessment that have
been set up by the LEA for the statementing of pupils with special
educational needs and what is expected of the school before those
processes are put into operation.

This points to action at two levels, one being the school's responsibility and the other that of the Local Education Authority.

What the school can do

Make your governors welcome in the school. If the governor has
taken the trouble to come into school make sure he or she is not
confined to the headteacher's office. No matter what the reason for
their visit at some time or other the head should say, 'Would you
like to look around?' or better still, 'Would you like to visit some
of the classes?'

If a governor has taken the trouble to come into your classroom
try to integrate him or her into its organisation. Try to avoid putting
them at the back of the room as you might an inspector. The
governor will almost certainly prefer it if he or she is made part of
the lesson and is given something to do.

Introduce the governor to the pupils and tell them about a
governor's duties. The way you do this will depend on the age of
your children. The explanation that you offer to year 10 pupils will
be very different from that given to year 2 pupils. As a good and

experienced teacher, you will know at what level it should be pitched. The children should be made to feel that the governor, although not often seen by them, is part of the school organisation, is working together with the head and staff to create an efficient school, and has their interests at heart.

There are many activities in the school, and especially in the SEN departments of secondary schools, to which governors should be invited. Coffee mornings, project presentations, plays, school visits, all are opportunities for the governor to get to know the children, the staff and above all feel part of the school.

If there is an INSET day that has special educational needs on the agenda then make sure the governing body is aware of it and that they are given an opportunity to join in. Governors find these days most interesting and add a whole new dimension to the subject by questioning from a different viewpoint to that of the teacher. This exercise is well worth the effort.

The LEAs responsibilities

Ensure that there is a governor or a pair of governors who have been nominated to take a specific interest in special educational needs. It would be desirable if those governors, or any other interested governor, attended a course on special educational needs. These courses are run by the local education authority and information can be gained from the governor training section of your LEA or the support service for special educational needs.

The nominated governor or governors should make a point of visiting the school with the specific purpose of finding out and understanding how the school provides for children with special educational needs. Some counties (e.g. Berkshire) have a 'Governor of the Month' scheme where one governor a month is nominated to visit the school and find out as much as he or she can about the staff and pupils. This avoids the embarrassing situation of a school being over-run with interested governors.

Invite a member of the special educational needs support service or an adviser with responsibility for special educational needs to speak to the governing body.

The Local Education Authority will have a monitoring and evaluation programme. Reports will be issued following any visit by the monitoring and evaluation team. Special educational needs is sure to feature as part of their reports and this should be considered by the governing body as soon as possible after the report is issued.

Ensure that each governor is aware of the formula that the LEA uses to identify the school's special educational needs in order to allocate funding under LMS.

Ensure that special educational needs is on the agenda of every meeting and ask the headteacher or the coordinator for special educational needs to present a report to the governing body. This report should be sent to all governors prior to the meeting so that the information that is contained in it may be digested and questions arising from the report can be formulated.

Areas of concern that may arise

Most schools will have children who require specialist help but do not carry a statement. The support for these children must be funded through LMS allocation. LEAs should have some criteria for identifying these pupils built into their LMS scheme. Usually the formula will contain consideration of the number of pupils who have free school meals (this has been a very contentious issue for many schools). Sometimes they will also consider a county-wide screening test which identifies pupils with special needs (e.g. Gloucestershire's *Early Assessment of Special Education*). Whatever the formula, the school should make sure that the governors are aware of it. If the scheme is so tightly drawn as to eliminate the children with special needs in their school from extra funding, then it is up to them to try to persuade the LEA to modify its scheme next year.

It may be very tempting for the school to try to economise in the early years of LMS and it is feared by many in the world of special education that children with special needs might be an area where economies could be made. Suggestions have been made by headteachers to replace qualified staff with non-teaching assistants who work alongside staff coping with the extra demands that these pupils can make. Many of the classroom assistants are excellent, dedicated people. Teachers who are concerned about the child with special needs receiving 'specialist' or 'individual' help could enlist the help of the governor who must then ensure that the pupils' needs are really being met and that the expertise which is required to cope with such pupils is not dispensed with purely as an economic measure.

Other arrangements include giving teachers the extra time to teach the special needs pupils themselves. This will involve employing supply teachers or part-time teachers to take over the class whilst a teacher takes those pupils who need the extra attention. In some cases, the headteacher has taken on the responsibility for teaching the pupils with special needs. This scheme has much to commend it as the teacher will know exactly in which area of the curriculum the child will require help, also the pupil will be familiar with the teacher. Unfortunately, this system falls down and tends to suffer when there are staff shortages and the part-timer gets whisked away for supply elsewhere, or the headteacher has such a load of administration that the SEN period is shelved. If governors are made wholly aware of the strategies that are being employed they should satisfy themselves that special educational needs have a high priority and are not marginalised in the ways mentioned above.

Cross-curricular issues

It is generally accepted that the National Curriculum as it stands leaves out very many important facets of a child's education. Amongst these facets are social and health education and careers guidance. These areas of the curriculum have always been regarded as very important for the child of low attainment. First and foremost, it is the teachers' responsibility to see that these cross-curricular themes are being covered. The SEN coordinator should be checking regularly to see that pupils with special needs are getting the SHE and career guidance that they have received in years prior to the introduction of the National Curriculum. Any problem in this area should primarily be dealt with at departmental level. If the problem persists through intransigence or lack of available resources, questions should be asked at governor level. The curriculum, resources, staffing and the numbers of pupils who are missing out should then be examined and the headteacher should be required to present a plan whereby provision can be made. In this way, the staff will be resourced fairly and in proportion to the problem presented to the whole school.

Access to the curriculum for pupils with SEN

The Education Reform Act 1988 gives all children access to the National Curriculum. It is the governors' duty to see that the school is doing all in its power to provide that access. In the past, children with special needs have been withdrawn from classes. Sometimes they were withdrawn from whole areas of the curriculum in order that their needs, mainly in literacy skills, could be met. Only if the governors are aware of the strategies used by the school will they be able to ensure that any disapplication of the National Curriculum is supported by a statement of special educational needs or a temporary direction made by the headteacher.

Disapplication of the National Curriculum

There will be some pupils for whom certain parts of the National Curriculum may not be appropriate. For instance a pupil who has to rely on technological aids to produce written work will not be able to achieve statements of attainment in the handwriting attainment target of the English curriculum. There are obvious implications for pupils who are blind or who have communication difficulties. Most of these 'disapplications' will be written into the pupil's statement.

However, a headteacher may find it necessary to make a 'temporary exception'. It is anticipated that this will be a rare occurrence. The temporary exception of any part of the National Curriculum can only be for six months before it is reviewed. The headteacher is required to inform the governing body of any temporary exception that he or she has made.

The headteacher must also inform the parents concerned. If the parents disagree with the headteacher the governors are required to listen to the parents' case and if necessary instruct the headteacher to lift the disapplication. If the governors agree with the headteacher's decision the parents may then go through the LEA complaints procedure.

Trouble could arise here if the governors have not been informed of the disapplication right from the start and been kept informed of the alternative strategies which have been employed to meet the pupil's needs. The governors cannot be expected to work in a vacuum.

Modification of the National Curriculum

Some modifications to the pupil's access to the National Curriculum will be written clearly into the pupil's statements of his or her special educational needs. Modification can also be made for pupils who are mainly taught programmes of study within the range of levels appropriate to their Key Stage. So a pupil who is not yet ready for Level 2 in certain attainment targets may be taught at Level 1 for part of the time.

It has also been suggested (Circular 15/89 para 36) that pupils may be moved up or down a Key Stage for a particular subject which will require a different teaching group where the majority of the pupils may be older or younger. Modifications of this nature should be reported to the governing body by the headteacher. Governors should ask at every governors' meeting if any further modifications or disapplications have been made.

Dealing with parents

Parents can often be seen as a stumbling block to statementing. If the parent becomes unreasonable and obstructive in the process it is almost certainly due to insensitive handling, poor communication or lack of information at vital stages either on the part of the LEA or the school. The governors' support can be enlisted here but only if they have been made fully conversant with the school's policy for identification, assessment and provision for SEN contained in the School Development Plan where there should be a requirement for the parent to be consulted at every stage of determining special provision.

Some schemes that have tried to help in governor training

There is no doubt that with all these increased responsibilities some sort of provision for training should be made. Some governor training packs have been published but no sooner does the pack hit the open market than it is outdated by yet more legislation. In the mid-1980s the government encouraged governor training through the Education Support Grants (ESGs) and the 1986 Education Act required LEAs to provide governor training. In response, many authorities have set up governor training sections through their INSET structure.

It may be helpful to see how two authorities, one urban and the other a very rural county LEA, have approached the task of making governors aware of the issues regarding special educational needs and, most importantly, of keeping them up-dated on these issues.

Urban area

In the urban area (a London borough), the governor training group was set up as early as January 1986 as an offshoot to the main Governor Training Advisory Group. Its aims were to raise a general awareness in all governors and then to target the 'named' governors for special needs for more specific training.

The first session was given a high profile by inviting a nationally known speaker who spoke about educational opportunity for all. The session was opened and closed by the Director of Education and as well as opportunities to discuss various aspects of special educational needs, each of the 100 governors who attended went away with comprehensive information packs.

The second session, the 'launch evening', was again given high profile by inviting a guest speaker and, once again, a binder full of materials for their personal follow-up reading was distributed.

The third session was again a Saturday and was much more of a participatory session including role-play of governor's meetings, studying case-notes and fictitious curriculum documents in order to raise specific issues with which governors may become involved.

In 1987, the governing bodies were required to name governors with a responsibility for SEN, to identify their training needs and to include SEN on all their future agendas. In May 1988, the specific SEN training was offered. These sessions were aimed at clarifying and exploring with governors what their special functions could and should be. When the 'function description' had been evolved, it was then used as a 'reference point for general discussion, for teaching purposes and as a peg for action'. (Wolfendale *et al.* 1990). Governors were able to formulate questions that could be taken back to their own governing bodies. These served as an aide-mémoire in an attempt to encourage them to take SEN issues seriously and to promote action.

Rural area

This area began formal governor training in 1990. The Advisory Teacher for Governor Training, who worked through the county INSET structure, had a good network of well-established Special Educational Needs Area Resource Centres (SENARCS) on which to base her training sessions. Each SENARC had a curriculum development teacher for special educational needs, at least one advisory teacher of the hearing impaired and an advisory teacher for the visually impaired. Also attached to each SENARC was a Senior Area Coordinator (SACSEN) whose duties included the overseeing of hospital tuition, home tuition and the provision of teachers for statemented pupils in mainstream schools. From these, a team of two curriculum development teachers, the heads of the hearing and visually impaired services and one SACSEN was formed to design a county-wide governor training programme for SEN.

It was decided that the areas that needed to be covered were:

1. to provide a broad view of special educational needs;
2. to examine a governor's responsibility in law, and suggest ways of fulfilling those responsibilities;
3. to examine the implications of local financial management on resourcing for SEN, and how such children might suffer;
4. to explain the role of the support services.

It was felt that the training sessions had to be given a professional and high profile atmosphere, therefore the team developed a pack of overhead projector transparencies which were well produced with a distinctive 'SEN governor training' logo.

The next step was for the team to train the trainers and an evening was organised when advisory staff from all the SENARCS had an opportunity to go through the OHP transparencies, to ask questions and to formulate their own team approach.

As it is such a rural area, schools tend to be far apart and small but keen to participate in any training initiative that brings them in contact with others. Schools are therefore clustered for training amongst other things. It was decided to operate on the basis of these clusters. Some research had been done by the governor training section into the best time for these sessions. Each cluster was offered one evening session of two hours, over a period beginning in November 1990 and ending in March 1991, by which time all the LEA schools would be managing their own budgets.

Further sessions were then offered on a governor training menu issued by the governor training section, being available to school governing bodies on an individual basis. In these sessions, it was possible for advisory staff who were familiar with a school's particular problem to address specific queries.

Other initiatives

There have been many initiatives from many different counties. For instance two counties have joined together in financing a video. They have employed a professional company to do the filming and the end product is a very well produced video which can be divided up into sections and used to spark off discussion and raise relevant issues. The BBC have also produced training packs with a video element.

Points arising from governor training initiatives

Governors are not teachers. They may be ignorant of issues regarding special educational needs but they are invariably keen to learn. Their time is precious, they too have jobs during the day which may well be as demanding as a teacher's. It is therefore important to give a great deal of thought to any training initiatives.

If too much emphasis is put on to theoretical principles, many governors will be dissatisfied as they require knowledge of their own school or local authority. They can read at their leisure about basic principles of being governors but local issues are harder for them to come to terms with without the people involved being available to answer their questions. Give any initiative a high profile and make the presentation as professional as possible.

Governor training will have to take place either in the evening or at weekends and a great deal of commitment is required from the trainers. Above all, don't waste the governors' time by delivering irrelevant information, by utilising too much role play or watching videos that do not deal with local issues. Governors need facts and relevant advice appertaining to their own situation. Having said that, perhaps the motto for all boards of governors should be 'Learn by other people's mistakes, not one's own'. Therefore, a chance to look at what other counties are doing and an opportunity to talk to other governors should be available.

Some questions to which governors need an answer

- What is meant by 'special educational needs'?
- How many pupils will have special educational needs?
- What is a statement of special educational needs?
- What should the school do before requesting a formal assessment?
- How should the school deal with a statemented pupil?
- From where does the money come to resource teaching of statemented pupils?
- What do I do if a parent complains about SEN provision?
- What is the duty of the LEA to pupils with SEN?
- What can governors do in order to meet legal requirements?
- What can governors do that will help them discharge their duties?

References and further reading

DES *Education Act 1980* London: HMSO.
DES *Education Act 1981* London: HMSO.
DES *Education Act 1986* London: HMSO.
DES *Education Reform Act 1988* London: HMSO.
DES (1989) *From Policy to Practice* London: DES.
DES (1989) Circular 15/89: *The Education Reform Act 1988: Temporary exceptions to the National Curriculum* (also Regulations) London: DES.
DES (1978) *Special Educational Needs* (The Warnock Report) London: HMSO.
Dodd, M. (1989) 'Governor training and special education' in *Support for Learning* 4, 2.
National Curriculum Council (1989) Circular No 5: *Implementing the National Curriculum — Participation by Pupils with Special Educational Needs.*
National Curriculum Council (1989) Guidelines 2: *A Curriculum for all.*
Wolfendale, S. *et al.* (1990) 'Governors and special educational needs: A collaborative in-service training programme with reference to the involvement of educational psychologists' in *Educational and Child Psychology* 7, 2.

Acknowledgements

The author wishes to acknowledge the help given by Jane Watkinson from the Governor training section and the advisory and support service of Gloucestershire Education Authority.

16 Talking with parents of 'dyslexic' children: the value of skilled discussion methods

John Acklaw and Yash Gupta

Conflict between a school and the parents of a 'dyslexic' child is quite often the result of difficulties in communication rather than any real difference of opinion between them about the reality or severity of a problem. Both parents and teachers will share a common aim of wanting the pupil to succeed. The school's aim will be to achieve this in partnership with the parents. Teachers will be most likely to establish this partnership through an understanding of the parents' frame of reference, and through the process of skilled discussion.

Problem of definition

The term 'dyslexia' has its origins in the medical profession. Originating in this context the word retains its medical connotations with its assumptions that it is an underlying physical condition which can be diagnosed differentially from other learning difficulties, and which may respond to specific prescriptions for treatment.

In fact, the British Medical Association has advised that the diagnosis and treatment of dyslexia are psychological and educational problems, not medical ones. Many local education authorities therefore prefer to follow the recommendations of the Tizard Committee (1972) and use the term *specific learning difficulty* rather than dyslexia. One way of describing it could be as follows:

> A child can be said to have a specific learning difficulty if he or she is experiencing *greater difficulty* in acquiring one or some of the skills, usually in the area of literacy or mathematics, than he or she experiences in other areas of the curriculum. This is a *heterogeneous* group of children whose only unifying feature is their difficulty in acquiring specific skills. *No assumption should be made about a single cause for these difficulties.*

If one accepts the above it is a recognition that a problem exists. Further than this, one of the authors found that a representative group of primary headteachers were able to describe the following characteristics in children who they knew had specific difficulties in learning to read, write, spell or calculate:

1. good in conversational skill and reasoning;
2. problems in auditory or visual memory — poor recall;
3. difficulties in sequential ordering of letters, numbers;
4. confusion in left – right directions;
5. reversal of certain letters and numbers;
6. history of late speech and language development;
7. poor coordination —usually clumsy in movements;
8. poor presentation of written work;
9. slow speed of writing;
10. bizarre spelling.

Not all children with specific learning difficulty have all these characteristics. Similarly, there are some children who seem to have a number of similar characteristics but master the skills of literacy and numeracy by the age of 8 or 9 years of age.

It would seem then that, despite differences in preference for the use of the term 'dyslexia', there is common ground that a minority of children have specific learning difficulties and that the characteristics of these children can be identified by schools. To this extent it is clear that teachers are able to share a common framework with parents who have obtained a diagnosis of dyslexia for their child.

If conflicts of view do arise, they are likely to occur where the school is asked by the parent to accept a diagnosis or assessment in which the school has played no part and which in some fundamental way conflicts with the approval of the school.

Schools in one area of an authority began to receive large numbers of independently produced reports from parents. Heads expressed concern about the following features found in them.

1. They contained too much psychological jargon.
2. They presented too limited a view of the children's functioning and stressed 'within child factors', not enough account being taken of possible environmental factors affecting the child's progress.
3. They equated IQ too closely with attainment. Teachers are beginning to appreciate that IQ scores are not an explanation of performance, or lack of it, in other areas of achievement.
4. Reports often appeared to respond to the needs of the parents for explanations of the child's achievement or lack of it. Contradictory facts would be used to draw similar conclusions in different cases.
5. Many of the recommendations took no account of what went on in the school or were unrealistic and not practical from the teacher's point of view.

These typical reservations present headteachers with a dilemma concerning how to enter into a sensible and constructive discussion with parents whose concerns for their children have motivated them to acquire these reports, often at a financial cost to themselves. The assessments upon which such reports are based are, and indeed should be, a trigger for discussion between the school and the parents. It is here that principles of skilled discussion can be useful (Fisher and Ury 1982).

Using the principles of skilled discussion

The first step in skilled discussion is to understand the barriers in communication that can exist between parties.

1. One barrier might be a straightforward conflict of belief concerning the existence of dyslexia as a condition which distinguishes the child's needs from those of other children with reading and spelling difficulties. The problem here is that any argument designed to persuade the parents that dyslexia does not exist, or that its existence is scientifically unproven, is to argue against a very strong belief system. By their nature,

belief systems are supported by faith, not rational proof, and so little is likely to be achieved by trying to persuade parents not to believe in this concept. Conflict will be avoided and a path to constructive argument opened by a recognition that a problem exists, whatever the interpretation of the cause.

2.   A difficult barrier for schools to overcome is that caused by a possible difference of view about the methods needed to assist the child. To the more enlightened primary school the methods routinely recommended in reports brought to them by parents will appear to be somewhat limited and prescriptive, and out of tune with the general approach of the school. However, blunt rejection alone would be unproductive. More helpful is a show of willingness to consider them while illustrating how children with learning difficulties can receive systematic teaching of specific skills within an enriched curriculum.

3.   Parents who have consulted outside experts in dyslexia may come to the school with a belief that their children need to be taught by teachers with a special kind of expertise not available within the school. This can be threatening or deskilling, especially as it is unlikely to be true. Again, attempting to deny the parents' belief is likely to be less productive than making clear your faith in the teaching skills available to the child and explaining what they are.

4.   The fourth barrier is the barrier of prejudice. If the parents are coming to the discussion with preconceptions, you at least can approach the problem with an open mind. Show an understanding that a problem exists even if the interpretations differ. Work from the basis that the parents' concern is real, and not that they are simply awkward or overanxious.

The second step is to examine whether your objective in meeting the parents is to achieve a situation where you both gain, or whether it is perceived as a potential 'win or lose battle'. Some parents may indeed see their objective in these terms but research suggests that the best negotiators seek an outcome in which each side feels that a gain has been made (that is, an 'I win — you win' outcome). The benefits to the school of this approach are that relationships are maintained on a constructive plane, and hostility is avoided in a situation where the school and parents may have to live with each other for several years.

A third step is to prepare for your discussion by considering how you might work within the following principles which have been shown to be effective in negotiations.

1. *Separate the people from the problem.* Consider the problem neutrally. Define it objectively, clarify it with the parents, agree it and disassociate it in your minds from personalities involved.
2. *Make the goal a wise outcome, reached amicably and efficiently.* As suggested above, you may have to live with parents for some years.
3. *Offer to proceed independently of trust.* You would like them to have faith in you but there is no particular reason why they should. Therfore, instead of giving them general assurances that you will do your best, suggest how they and you can review what action has been taken. Agree clear actions that can be verified and set dates for a joint review.
4. *Reason and explore.* Be open to reason but do not respond to threats. Do not feel you need to have a position which must be defended. Try to invent options for solutions to the problem under discussion.

Lastly, to be effective, it is essential to prepare carefully for any meeting. Taking into account the points already made, preparation would include the following actions.

1. Think through the problems as they affect you and as they affect the parent. Thinking about the parents' problems in advance enables you to signal to them that you are considering them and are attempting to look at the issues from their point of view and not only from your own. This is a sign that you view the discussion as a joint exercise in problem solving and not a confrontation.
2. What are your mutual interests? Clearly you both want to feel that you are achieving the best for the child. It is in your mutual interest to maintain a good working relationship and collaborate to meet the child's needs. By identifying mutual interests, you are likely to make the parents allies in the discussion rather than adversaries.
3. What facts do you need to have? Make sure that you have them before you start. Facts are objective; being willing to look at and share the facts of the child's needs and the steps taken to meet them helps to ensure that the discussion is a reasoned one between adults and not simply an exchange of unhelpful opinions and suppositions about the nature of the problem.
4. What are your objectives for the meeting? What outcome will you aim for? You will want the discussion to move in a positive direction towards agreement if possible, but at the very least

towards an understanding of each other's views. Describe your intended objectives in terms of action that you would wish to see the parent and yourself taking as a result of the meeting.

Conclusion

There is a general expectation that schools and parents should work in partnership to meet children's needs. The partnership concept was given particular emphasis and applicability to children with special educational needs by the Warnock Report (1978) and consequent legislation. However, partnership can be difficult to maintain where misunderstanding or differing views arise as a consequence of differing interpretations or the use of labels to describe the child's needs. This paper has attempted to suggest how better understanding and communication might be achieved between schools and the parents of children who have been labelled dyslexic.

References

DES (1972) *Children with Specific Reading Difficulties* (The Tizard Report) London: HMSO.
DES (1978) *Special Educational Needs* (The Warnock Report) London: HMSO.
Fisher, R. and Ury, W. (1982) *Getting to Yes: Negotiating agreement without giving in* London: Hutchinson.

Part VI
Staff development

17 In-service courses: staff development and special educational needs

John Visser

Teacher education, in-service and staff development are undergoing changes. To those of us who have been in education for any length of time, this may not be anything new. Tinkering with the education system appears to be part of the British way of doing things. However, these present changes have been very far reaching in their effects. They encompass the type and length of pre-service training, the provision, length and delivery of in-service courses, and the role of teachers in their own training.

Teacher training

The change to a four year BEd teacher education programme is now complete, together with the requirement that two years of the course be devoted to study in a subject discipline to levels commensurate with a university undergraduate course. This demand, whatever its merits, has effectively cut professional training to two years. Initial training via a PGCE is now a 36 week course. The extra six weeks has been largely taken up with more school practice. The content of courses is governed by CATE, the Council for the Accreditation of Teacher Education, who issue circulars known as CATE Notes by which they govern the content of pre-service training. Amongst the content required is an element of special educational needs. However it is but one element amongst a number which teacher education courses have to cover. There are further constraints on the time available for teacher education. In effect teachers are trained either by following a 36 week PGCE course or a four year course of which two years are devoted to study of a subject at normal undergraduate level. This really only leaves 60 weeks to train teachers. Thus special education as a topic is a requirement in initial training but the amount of time available for it is severely limited. HMI have indicated (1990) that the effect of this has been for many courses to permeate SEN across other subjects and that this has not been very satisfactory.

However there is some certainty that new entrants to the profession will have some notion of individual differences and learning difficulties. Training institutions will vary in the emphasis they give to special educational needs in their courses. Some probationers will have a detailed knowledge and understanding of children with special educational needs. They will have examined their teaching skills and incorporated aspects of differentiation into their delivery of the curriculum in such a manner that all the children in their classes will have their educational needs met. On the other hand, an awareness of the 1981 Act, and what an educational psychologist looks like, may well be the sum total of other probationers' pre-service courses.

There remains a need for initial teacher education to provide a more universally agreed 'base' content of special educational needs. This would enable schools to be more certain of the amount of support they will need to provide to probationers who are working with children with special educational needs. In-service work would also benefit, the providers of INSET would have a base upon which to build.

Changes in INSET provision

In-service provision has undergone radical changes over the past five years and further changes are still in the pipeline (Jones 1989). There is hardly an aspect of in-service work that has not been reviewed. Fundamental questions as to how, when and where in-service work should be provided and by whom have underpinned these changes. As we enter the mid-1990s, a further question is being asked more strongly. Is there a separate body of knowledge called 'special education' or is it all contained within issues concerned with good teaching practice and educational psychology? Jones (1989) when first raising

this issue poses no neat solutions or answers. It is a valid question
we should ask in special education. If special educators continue to
state that special education teaching is the same as good teaching
then we should not be too surprised if special educational needs
in-service courses disappear or are entirely subsumed in generalist
teacher education courses.

The most notable change has been that one year secondment
courses have almost disappeared, with only the mandatory courses
for teachers of children with sensory impairment remaining. There
was much that was wrong with the previous system of offering and
providing in-service courses. The 'pool' as it was known allowed
course providers to design and mount courses with DES approval for
which teachers could then apply. Local authorities would then apply
to the pool for reimbursement of a substantial proportion of the fees
and secondment costs. The results of this was that many in-service
courses were not school based, and were more 'academic research'
orientated. Based in institutions of higher education and run by
research-based lecturers, the teachers became passive recipients of
'distilled wisdom'. Teachers returning from a year's secondment
were as likely to be asked about their golf swing and told to forget
those half-baked ideas taught by those who couldn't teach. Their
colleagues were not eager to embrace new ideas, methods and
resources which a 'privileged' seconded colleague had imbibed at a
course centred at an institution for higher education. Teachers
considered themselves fortunate to obtain secondment once in their
careers.

Indeed, often as not, having completed a year's secondment, the
teacher concerned would gain promotion in another school, perhaps
in another authority. So whilst the overall quality of the profession
may have been improved for a few, their school and colleagues,
having suffered the disruption that secondment inevitably caused,
received none of the benefits. In highlighting some of the drawbacks
of the previous system, it should be remembered that it also had its
merits. If funding had allowed for more teachers to have a year's
secondment and more courses had been school-based then the
enhancement of teachers' skills would have been achieved.

The main merits of the long course, completed in a full-time
mode, are:

— the time which they allow for reflection by their students on
    their professional experience;
— the recharging of a teacher's enthusiasm after the teaching for
    a number of years;
— the space and opportunity to consider new ideas and
    approaches.

Funding for INSET

Currently, in-service provision is in a very transitory stage. It has gone through GRIST (Circulars 6/86 and 7/86) LEAGTS (DES 1991a) and is now in GEST (DES 1991b). LEAs, themselves under threat as this chapter is written, are required to devolve almost the entire in-service budget to schools on a formula basis. The Secretary of State, through the DES, designates areas of in-service which will receive funding. However, this funding pays for only part of the total. It is percentage funding. The LEA has to find from its own funds a percentage of the costs. This varies for different areas of in-service but currently runs at an average of 60 per cent paid by the DES, the remainder being funded by the LEA. For SEN courses, the percentage is generally higher at 65 per cent. It should be borne in mind that this percentage has dropped in succeeding years from 90 per cent! What will happen in future is a matter of concern, and not just to those who provide courses. The effect of other government legislation such as rate-capping has taken a further toll on the monies available for in-service courses. If funding for courses falls still further, the provision of in-service will become non-viable for institutions and the number and range of courses will diminish still further.

This shift of funds directly to the schools has meant that there has been a radical shift in the focus of in-service work. Schools are now a little more choosey over the courses on which they will send their teachers. With limited funds they need to ensure that they obtain the greatest return for the maximum number of staff with the least outlay. This might have a deleterious effect on future professional development programmes.

It is the payee who calls the tune under these arrangements. The shift in financing, together with the lack of impact of the old-style, one-year courses has led to a demand for shorter courses which are school-based. Part-time courses which have an assignment that carries benefits for the school are now much in evidence as a result. These are seen as having more potential for providing both for the professional development of the teacher and for the teacher's school. This professional development not only enhances the teacher's skills but also provides that teacher with the ideas, knowledge and understanding to effect change in his or her school.

There are two major problems with the present arrangement besides the overall insufficiency of the funding. The first is that, by devolving the limited funds down to each school, the actual amount a school has is insufficient to 'buy' long part-time courses for, in many cases, even one teacher. The largest part of the cost for a school which sends a teacher on a course during term time is that of supply cover. This prevents them from being able to support teachers on full-time courses of even 20 days' duration. The monies are usually devolved on a per capita basis and most schools are relatively small. This is particularly so in the case of special schools, where some of the most highly specialised training is needed. There will be particular problems in schools for children with severe learning difficulties as the Government has now stopped the training of teachers for these children through an initial teacher training route.

The second major problem is that whilst the schools and LEAs have been grappling with these changes in funding, the providing institutions have been coping with funding changes as well. They now receive only 90 per cent of their funds from their funding bodies. The remaining ten per cent has to made up from what is known as 'income generation'. In education faculties this can only come from research grants, consultancies and non-award bearing courses. This puts pressure on providing institutions to devise ever smaller modules which can be taken by teachers who can perhaps save them up to cash in for an award. This further fragmenting of in-service courses reduces the possibility of teachers obtaining overall coherent staff development.

The changes in provision have not therefore meant more, or even better, courses for serving teachers. Warnock's indication of one in five children having special educational needs has never been seriously questioned. Indeed, in many schools the staff would point out that it is a serious underestimate. With the long overdue introduction of an entitlement curriculum, teachers are now having to face the challenge of how to teach a broad and balanced curriculum to the full range of children in their schools. Pre-service training has, in many cases, been woefully inadequate in this area. Schools are now addressing this issue through whole-school policies. Whilst it has become more professionally relevant, in-service training still has a number of constraints. The need for in-service courses in the field of special educational needs remains high. Indeed, the survey by Clunies-Ross and Wimhurst (1983) would still hold good if repeated today. Even amongst those who have direct responsibility for special education needs there are too few who have had any specialist training.

Crystal ball gazing

To summarise, new teachers are entering the profession with differing levels of awareness and knowledge of special educational needs. There is a teaching force which has received little or no input concerning special educational needs in their training, and there is a large number of teachers with responsibility for special educational needs in both mainstream and special schools who are without any specialist training. The finances, never sufficient, are now further stretched by being spread very thinly amongst all teachers and are under further threat from the Government. The providers of in-service need to look very carefully at the fees which they charge as they have to raise more of their income from in-service work. In-service continues in a state of flux. What then, is the way forward? It is a brave or very foolish writer who makes prophesies! Since I have never aspired to the former it must be the latter which underpins what follows. Crystal ball gazing at the best of times in education is a dangerous occupation. The thoughts which follow are but one way forward. They are derived partly from experience across a wide range of in-service provision and partly from a conviction that some of the suggestions are essential if we are to raise standards and if children are to benefit from better teaching.

Future provision for pre-service courses

In pre-service courses the special educational needs input must be related directly to the classroom situation. These courses should concentrate on learning strategies and aspects of individual differences which impinge upon teachers' responsibilities in delivering the entitlement curriculum (Barthorpe and Visser 1991). Thomas and Smith (1985) argue for three criteria upon which to judge the content of such a course. They are contained in the following questions:

1. Does the content of the course give a deeper understanding of how to help pupils whose learning strategies are inappropriate? Does it advise on the management of difficult and disruptive pupils?
2. Does it focus upon the most commonly encountered learning and behavioural problems?
3. Does it relate practice, policy and perspectives to school situations which have immediate relevance to students?

These three criteria give a base to possible special educational needs input in pre-service work which could then form a basis for planning in-service courses. If these aims were achieved, it would enable probatitioners to have a leavening effect in those schools to which they were appointed upon completion of their training. In-service courses could then lead on from this to provide a range of experiences which, if correctly structured, would support a more coherent professional development and career for teachers within special education. One such structure has been proposed by Hinson *et al.* (1985). Given this model, courses could be tailored to meet the individual requirements of teachers involved with children who have special educational needs along a continuum from awareness courses to advanced courses dealing with management and policy. Such courses could be based securely within the sector of the profession in which the teacher serves. It would also emphasise the fact that it is 'initial' teacher training.

A different view of INSET

What is required is a spiral view of in-service education rather than the 'once-and-for-all' model that the pool arrangements promoted. Teachers must be given opportunities to enhance their skills as they progress through their careers. Opportunities should also exist for those teachers who remain in a particular post for a major proportion of their career, because they require refresher and top-up courses which would enable them to keep abreast of developments. Courses, however practical or academically high-flown, should be planned on the basis that the teacher is there to enable children to learn.

Previous in-service work could be likened to dropping a pebble into a pond and hoping that the ripples would have some effect. Future arrangements for in-service work must act rather like a honey pot attracting a teacher's colleagues. The honey pot must have two attractive dimensions: the content of a course must be professionally relevant, and it needs to be delivered in a professional manner. In-service must enable teachers to enhance their skills, understanding and knowledge in order that they will be able to meet the special educational needs of individuals. This will only come about if the work is keyed into the school where colleagues can become actively engaged in the work that students are undertaking. This engagement could take many different forms, from discussion and joint projects to a variety of other interactive learning activities. Courses which are seen to have direct relevance to teachers are the ones which will effect most change.

Longer courses will be required by teachers as they develop their careers. The model suggested by Hinson *et al.* (op cit) is one which is capable of incorporating the developing role of the special needs post holder. This role will always be an evolving one because, unlike other curriculum post holders, it has no subject base upon which to rest. The role is essentially one which is engaged in enhancing teaching strategies and learning skills. The model suggested is a dynamic and developing one for special educational needs teachers in their work as support or collaborative teachers. Seven broad aspects are indicated as part of this role and all implicitly require the facilitation of staff development alongside the provision of in-service courses.

It is important to stress that in-service should not cease as soon as a teacher has gained promotion to a managerial position such as that of headteacher, adviser, or head of support service. Indeed, it could be argued that in-service and staff development becomes even more important. Too often in the past, staff development and in-service have been left to 'on-the-job-training', an unsatisfactory state of affairs when the pressure to do the job all too often absorbed all available time. As a result, the chance to reflect, evaluate and absorb present practice and new ideas was seldom achieved.

If the status and professionalism of the teachers within special educational needs are to be raised a range of courses, from awareness to advanced work on policy and management, is required. Many of these courses whilst having a core or focus which is 'special' should draw upon the work going on in the other fields of education. For example, courses in management in special education should draw upon the skills and knowledge being offered in other courses in educational needs are to be raised a range of courses, from awareness them.

Disseminating research

The emphasis on school-based training must not be allowed to smother other aspects of in-service work, such as the dissemination of research. Traditionally, research in education has been despised by the vast majority of the profession. It has variously been seen as telling teachers what they already know, being so esoteric as to have no relevance to the teacher's classroom, or being so entwined with the researcher's jargon and statistics that its point is lost in a maze of words and numbers. Just occasionally it has been accused of having all three faults! Journal editors are well aware that few teachers read their articles, particularly those containing the results of research. Even the *Times Educational Supplement* continues to advertise itself in terms of its usefulness in finding a new job, rather than in enabling teachers to keep abreast of educational developments. One function of in-service courses must be to enable teachers to see the relevance of research and engage in it themselves. Research will need to be demystified in order to achieve this. In fact, research is an activity which teachers undertake daily whenever they plan, execute, evaluate and analyse a course of action in teaching.

More action type research is being fostered on courses, thus enabling
the dissemination of good practice.

Modular courses

One effect of the legislative and financial changes is the modularisa-
tion of courses. Courses which previously were of a year's duration
have now been divided into modules, each module becoming a self-
contained course. Teachers follow a variety of these modules to
gain eventually an award of some description. Amongst the merits
of this system is the possibility for teachers to build up their award
from modules which meet their particular individual needs. In this
writer's view, one of the dangers is that teachers build up an
imbalanced array of modules which does not adequately reflect their
needs, since neither they nor the school have clearly identified them.
Guidance from staff development officers and course providers
needs to be available to enable teachers to avoid this trap. A second
danger is the assumption that the acquisition of knowledge, skills
and understanding can be accomplished merely by putting together
small discrete units taught by different tutors. If it is to be meaningful, all learning requires motivation and inspiration as well as
access to the knowledge, skills and understanding required. Even
resource-based learning, such as that delivered by the Open University, relies heavily on interactions between teacher and taught. Most
of us are indebted to individual tutors and teachers who, over a long
period of time, have provided the inspiration and the motivation to
try new ideas, to face challenges and to implement changes in
schools and classroom. Short modules taught by different tutors,
with little time allowed for building relationships, will diminish this
important aspect of staff development in in-service work. If the
course has a large percentage of time given to school-based work,
this will be heightened. In the worst cases teachers could gain an
award in special education needs without ever having attended a
seminar or lecture, let alone having had an opportunity to discuss
their thoughts and ideas with their peers.

Distance learning

Distance learning courses, like part-time courses, have much to offer
the hard-pressed budget since they are relatively inexpensive and
incur no teacher supply costs. Good distance learning courses
break down the isolation of the 'long distance' learner by offering
group tutorials and summer schools as well as some sort of help-line.
However, these courses are essentially for highly motivated teachers

who prefer to work through materials largely by themselves. They also need to be confident learners with good study skills. Given these attributes and a personal tutor system which provides clear, fast and accurate feedback to students, distance learning courses can provide useful in-service courses and staff development opportunities. Shrinkage in the overall numbers of special education tutors and courses means that this form of in-service is set to increase during the next few years.

Keeping tutors up-to-date

There is now a requirement for tutors involved with the initial training of teachers to have recent and relevant experience of teaching in school. This requirement amounts to the equivalent of one term in every 15. Unfortunately, no such requirement has yet been made of those involved in in-service work. Nevertheless, the day of the higher education tutor who could not teach and so teaches others to teach is rapidly fading (if indeed it was ever as prevalent as some thought). What needs to be avoided, as LEA staff become more involved in providing in-service, is the replacement of the tutor who 'could not' by the LEA adviser, educational psychologist, or support teacher who 'cannot'. All those involved in the provision of in-service must have recent and relevant experience of the classroom if courses are to relate directly to the needs of teachers.

The teacher's role

What then is the teacher's role in staff development and in-service work? Teachers can no longer expect to be passive recipients. If the quality of staff development and in-service courses is to be enhanced and made professionally relevant, then teachers will need to be actively involved in course planning, delivery and evaluation. Courses should no longer be wholly prescriptive in content, didactic in delivery, with set answers to hypothetical questions. After all, when so many changes have taken place in schools following the 1988 Education Act, it is teachers who have experienced them. Teachers on courses should expect to become actively involved as researchers, and disseminators of good practice by undertaking assignments concerned with actual issues and problems within their own schools. This does not negate the need for courses to have a clear syllabus and well laid out content. There have been a number of comments in the *Times Educational Supplement* in recent years complaining about courses where teachers have just been put into groups and told to discuss an issue, reporting back to the whole group via the ubiquitous Flip Chart. On occasions this can be a very useful method but it requires substantial input upon which the discussion can build.

The second role for teachers lies in being involved with the determination of staff needs for particular in-service courses. Teachers should take an active part in this process. Only then will their needs be clearly articulated and stand a chance of being met. It might also ensure that the limited amount of money available for staff development days is spent efficiently. As someone who enjoys working with teachers in school and who has completed a large number of staff development days, I am amazed at the number of times I am asked to contribute to in-service courses without being briefed by those concerned as to what they wish to achieve. On one occasion, this stretched to being asked 'to do something' on special educational needs for a whole staff. When I enquired what was required, I was informed that they just want to know how to deal with these children and could I write a whole-school policy — and by the way, they usually started at 9.30 and were finished by 2pm! Obviously the school had not involved their special needs coordinator in the planning.

NARE (1990) deals with this issue, and others, in its booklet concerned with the planning of in-service and staff development courses. It indicates clearly the need for school training days to be planned within the framework of the school's development plan. As a starting point, the booklet highlights the need to obtain a staff's view regarding their training needs if a day is to be used effectively. The booklet stresses the need for such days to be part of a school policy which has evolved through consultation with all those concerned. Each course should have clear objectives, be well planned and delivered. Thorough evaluation is necessary in order that future courses can build upon present successes. The booklet goes on to deal with issues such as the choice of venue, methods of course delivery, the logistics of the day and other matters vital in organising successful school-based INSET.

The role of associations

The DES is responsible for the central direction of much of the in-service work which it funds. The precise mechanics of how these priorities are decided have not been made too explicit. However, professional associations can, and do, bring pressure to bear when they are made aware of the needs of their members. The individual teacher needs to be active in such associations because without an active and widely based membership, their role will diminish. With them will go a vital pressure group for the provision of in-service. These associations also provide staff development opportunities by holding short courses in the evenings and weekends. Their annual courses are usually held at Easter time. Meeting with like-minded professionals can be a potent source of ideas, providing the opportunity to share ways of meeting children's needs.

In conclusion

Perhaps my crystal ball gazing is too unrealistic. Real problems in providing in-service and staff development exist. Neither the current level of funding nor the opportunities available are sufficient to meet the demand for INSET in special needs. It is therefore important that the quality of the courses which are available is as high as possible. This chapter has argued for teachers to play their part in maintaining and enhancing these standards. Whatever the future holds, one thing is certain that teachers hold the key to the way in which their in-service training and staff development will progress.

References

Barthorpe, P. and Visser, J. (1991) *Differentiation: Your Responsibility* Stafford: NARE.

Clunies-Ross, L. and Wimhurst, S. (1983) *The Right Balance. Provision for Slow Learners in Secondary Schools* Windsor: NFER-Nelson.

DES (1986) Circular 6/86, *Approval of Courses for Further Training for School and Further Education Teachers in England 1987/88 and Notification of Intended Arrangements for 1988/89* London: HMSO.

DES (1990) *Special Educational Needs in Initial Teacher Training* London: HMSO.

DES (1991a) *The Implementation of the Local Training Grant Scheme* London: HMSO.

DES (1991b) *Grants for Education Support and Training, 1991–1992* London: HMSO.

Hinson, M. *et al.* (1985) NARE Guidelines No. 6: *Teaching Roles For Special Educational Needs* Stafford:NARE.

Jones, N. (1989) 'Needs and styles of in-service' in Davies, J.D. and Davies, P. *A Teacher's Guide to Support Services* London: NFER-Nelson.

National Association for Remedial Education (1982) *Guideline no. 4: In-service Education for Remedial Teachers* Stafford: NARE.

National Association for Remedial Education (1990) *Planning Your School-Based INSET* Stafford: NARE.

Thomas, D. and Smith, C. (1985) 'Special educational needs and initial training' in Sayer, J. and Jones, N. (eds.) *Teacher Training and Special Educational Needs* London: Croom Helm.

18 Classroom observation: a powerful tool for teachers?

Terence Bailey

> There is general agreement about the value of direct observation
> of classrooms but less agreement about the methodology for
> such observations.
>
> (P. Croll, *Systematic Classroom Observation*)

Although trainee teachers have long learnt their craft by observing
seasoned teachers in action, the value of classroom observation for
a range of purposes has been recognised more and more over the last
few years. In many cases the observation has been carried out by
visitors to the school, such as Her Majesty's Inspectors (HMI) and
local education authority (LEA) advisers but in other instances
teachers have observed colleagues.

HMI use observation as part of their inspections of a school.
Advisers and advisory teachers use observation as a means of assessing the competence of probationary teachers or to identify good
practice. Clustering groups of primary and secondary schools
together as a way of improving continuity between phases of education has led to visits of staff to observe colleagues working in another
phase. Volunteers like parents and governors also have an opportunity to build up a picture of what goes on in a school through
classroom observation. Educational psychologists use observation in

the classroom as part of their assessment of a pupil but they will also wish to know how the child interacts with the teacher. The collection of data through classroom observation has formed a major element in several recent major research projects.

The use of observation by teachers working with colleagues within their own schools is now recognised as important. The Report of the Appraisal Training Working Group of the Advisory, Conciliation and Arbitration Service (1986) emphasised that classroom observation should be an essential feature of appraisal. Many more senior managers in both mainstream and special schools now use classroom observation in the assessment of their staff. The move to in-class support in both primary and secondary schools has provided opportunities for teachers to observe each other and to provide constructive feedback about such issues as teaching and learning styles. In other instances, courses with a focus on action research in the classroom, such as Open University course E806, have opened the classroom door to teachers as researchers.

The requirement of the Education Reform Act to monitor and review the National Curriculum is likely to accelerate the practice of classroom observation as part of this process. However, the difficulties involved in the process are great. They are highlighted in 'Insight' from Charlotte Mason College (Summer 1990). The headteacher and deputy of a primary school wanted to use classroom observation as a way of identifying the school's INSET needs. The head wrote:

> My deputy and I felt the obvious solution was to devise a way in which evidence from classroom observation would form a basis of our INSET . . . We discussed who would observe in the classroom but it was not as easy as we thought. Some staff found it wasn't easy to make sense of the information confronting them. The difficulty was not in solving the problem but in knowing where the essence of the problem was in the first place.

The school ended up seeking help with the observations from college staff.

This article offers an approach to observation which can be used by staff in primary and special schools, by LEA officers, advisers and advisory teachers, psychologists or special needs support staff.

Approaches to classroom observation

The approaches adopted by researchers into what goes on in classrooms lie on a continuum between what can be called the *qualitative – quantitative dimension*.

Qualitative approach

At one end of the spectrum is the social anthropological approach, where you approach the classroom with no predetermined way of observing, and just 'observe'. Notes and anecdotal records are made of salient phenomena which strike you over a period of time. The record is usually a lengthy piece of descriptive writing.

Advantage: The observer can respond to what is going on by switching attention between individuals or different events.

Disadvantages: This approach is time consuming and haphazard, and it is difficult to know exactly what to record; no two observers record the same observations.

Quantitative or systematic approach

At the other end of the spectrum are those who feel that casual observation is disorganised and meaningless. In the quantitative approach the observer uses a systematic set of events (see Amidon and Hough 1967, Croll and Moses 1985, Flanders 1970, Galton, Simon and Croll 1980, Love and Roderick 1971, Merrett and Wheldall 1986). Records are often in the form of rating scales or numerical data which are computerised.

Advantage: There is a focus on specific aspects of the classroom in a more systematic way. Two observers can achieve higher inter-observer reliability.

Disadvantages: Recording only specific data with a simple coding system means other excellent data is lost. If the schedule it too complex to code, it can interfere with the observation.

An eclectic approach

Observation is time consuming and therefore we need to use the time as efficiently as possible to collect evidence. (Whatever misgivings one has about HMI 'hit and run' inspections of schools, their reports are always based on evidence observed.)

It is possible to combine elements of both the qualitative and the quantitative approaches outlined above. The checklist or nudge sheet in figure 18.1 has been developed over a number of years. It acts as an *aide-mémoire* and allows the observer to gather evidence about the main constituents within the classroom. Key comments by teachers and pupils and key behaviour by teacher or pupils are recorded.

The main constituents are the room itself, the learning materials, the learners and teachers.

The theoretical framework on which my nudge sheet is based relates in general to the work of effective primary schools (such as Mortimore *et al.* 1986), and in particular to classroom research on, for example, the management of classroom behaviour (Kounin 1970) and the analysis of verbal interaction (Flanders 1970).

It also includes coverage of three out of four of the variables outlined by Wragg (1983):

1. *Presage*: Personality, home background, intelligence, values, attitudes, previous experience of teachers and pupils.
2. *Process*: Teachers' use of praise, criticism, questioning, non-verbal behaviour (e.g. gesture and eye contact), deployment of ancillary assistant; also whether pupils engage in curriculum activities such as reading or a science experiment and non-task activity such as fooling around.
3. *Context*: Seating layout of room, size of room and physical features, length of lesson, materials used, number of pupils, time of day, display etc.
4. *Product*: Data recall, acquisition of concepts or skill by the child, understanding instructions etc.

Data on the presage variables in research is often collected by rating scales. (For example, for the teacher it might include a disciplinarian – *laissez faire* dimension). In my view these variables are open to too great a degree of subjectivity and they are not therefore recorded.

Using the checklist

Preliminary work

Carry out the following if possible before you go into a class to observe a teacher/colleague.

1. Have a preparatory meeting with the teacher/colleague to establish rapport.
2. Agree a mutually convenient time (date) for the observation to take place.
3. Seek data about the nature of the class — numbers, ages etc.

4. Establish the objective(s) of the work to be observed if possible.
5. Agree how you will be introduced to the class.
6. Agree a time for a follow-up discussion.
7. Establish whether the teachers'/colleagues' planning book will be available for you when you enter the classroom.
8. Advisers/advisory teachers should arrange, if appropriate, to seek the views of the headteacher or other senior staff on the work being undertaken in the classroom you visit. (In the current climate of teacher shortages it is essential to know whether the class has been taught by one teacher or a range of supply teachers. As Mortimore *et al.* (1986) highlighted, noise levels and pupil movement were higher and the amount of time a teacher spent interacting with the pupils was less where there were changes of teacher.)

Observing in the classroom

1. Initially examine the teacher's/colleague's planning book to identify:
    a. school/year group/individual planning for delivery of the National Curriculum;
    b. curriculum breadth, balance, relevance and differentiation;
    c. curriculum delivery (such as balance of themes/topics and additional skills work);
    d. evidence of cross-curricular planning.
2. Talk to the pupils when appropriate to identify what they are doing and why.
3. Look at the pupils' books, folders and records.
4. Talk to the teacher/colleague at an appropriate time during the lesson or at the end of the lesson to clarify observations, discuss events and so on.

Interpreting the nudge sheet

The process of combining different data to describe a situation from more than one perspective is called *triangulation*. Usually the three-way approach consists of teacher and pupil comments plus observers' evidence. Data collected by observation (for example, of teacher – pupil interaction) is strengthened when it is confirmed by talking to the teacher and pupil.

Triangulation involves gathering accounts of a teaching situation from three quite different points of view; namely, those of the

Name of teacher .... No. of pupils ....

Class .... Age range ....

The classroom as a working environment

1. Was the teacher in the classroom to meet the children?
2. Is there a set procedure for pupils coming in and leaving the classroom?
3. How did the teacher get pupils started on the task?
4. Were the materials to be used in the lesson organised, clearly labelled and ready for use?
5. What pattern of classroom organisation did you observe – individual, group, class teaching?
6. If team teaching or ancillary support was in evidence how did it work?
7. If parents were involved within the classroom how did it work?

Physical setting

1. How was classroom set out?
2. Does the classroom present a pleasant working environment?
3. Does the classroom layout help or hinder the children when carrying out their tasks?
4. How far did the display of pupils' work link with planning and delivery of the curriculum?
5. How far did the noise level impede pupils working?

Task-related factors

To what extent did pupil(s) :

1. understand the purpose of the lesson?
2. understand instructions?
3. show enthusiasm and interest in the work?
4. show a friendly, relaxed and confident attitude to the teacher?
5. cope adequately with the activities set?
6. reach an acceptable standard in the task(s) set?
7. know the procedures and routines of the classroom?
8. behave appropriately?
9. work co-operatively with other pupils?
10. refer to other pupils for help?
11. refer to additional material which might help?
12. move from one activity to another using set guidelines?

To what extent did the teacher

1. show a firm yet friendly, relaxed and encouraging attitude to the pupil(s)?
2. secure and retain the attention of the pupil(s) when necessary?
3. time the lesson/activity appropriately?
4. provide for progression in learning?
5. cope with differences in pupils' ability levels?
6. use praise and other forms of encouragement?

7. provide opportunities for pupils to take decisions about and responsibilities for their learning?
8. move around the classroom to assist or work with individual pupils/groups of pupils?
9. anticipate and avoid difficult behaviour?
10. deal with minor interruptions or a crisis in a firm but consistent manner?
11. allow pupils to comment on or mark their own work?
12. incorporate multicultural issues into her/his teaching?
13. demonstrate a variety of teaching methods?
14. provide clear instructions?
15. use unscripted incidents/comments by children to enhance learning?
16. use the curricular activities provided for the pupils to assess their progress?
17. use information technology as an integral part of teaching?

Communication issues

When communicating with the pupil(s), to what extent did the teacher

1. use vocabulary the children understood?
2. allow for maximum participation of the pupil(s)?
3. use clarifying questions?
4. ask higher order questions which encourage imaginative responses?
5. prompt when appropriate?
6. use pupil responses to encourage further discussions?
7. reword questions or answers to emphasise meaning?
8. use a clear, audible and interesting voice?
9. provide clear instructions which allowed pupils to work independently without continual recourse to the teacher?

Evidence

(When compiling the form leave sufficient space to complete this section.)

Figure 18.1 Nudge sheet for classroom observation

teacher, the pupils, and a participant observer. . . . Each point of the triangle stands in a unique epistemological position with respect to access to relevant data about a teaching situation. The teacher is in the best position to gain access via introspection to his/her own intentions and aims in the situation. The students are in the best position to explain how the teacher's actions influence the way they respond in the situation. The participant observer is in the best position to collect data about the observable features of the interaction between teachers and pupils. By comparing his/her own account with accounts from the two other standpoints, a person at one point of the triangle has an opportunity to test and perhaps revise it on the basis of more sufficient data (Hopkins and Bollington 1989).

In essence we wish to know:

1. Were suitable conditions established for learning to take place — opportunities for pupils to discuss, enquire, construct, create, make?
2. Were pupils able to access the materials easily in order to undertake the task(s) as independently as possible?
3. Were the activities suitable for the children's ages and stage of learning and/or for their social development?
4. Was the classroom climate such that pupils spent most of their time on task with support where appropriate, rather than exhibiting behaviour problems?
5. Were there opportunities for pupils to talk, discuss and develop language?

Some cautions

1. The biggest problem about observation is the observer. We all carry around attitudes, prejudices and biases which affect what we see. Beware of the halo effect. Clean, well-dressed children tend to create positive feelings in the viewer. Unclean, unkempt children may generate negative feelings in the viewer. This can affect interpretation. Research using rating scales shows behaviour of the former may not be marked as such, since inappropriate behaviour is forgiven. Similar behaviour of the latter group is marked down.
2. The presence of an observer, particularly in a short, one-off session, can actually alter the situation to the extent that you may not be observing the 'norm' for the classroom. Some

research suggests that there is more child-orientated behaviour by the teacher when an observer is present.

3. The period of observation is limited to a snapshot in time. In describing what we see we will be doing the teacher a disservice if we fail to remember that teaching has gone on prior to the visit and will go on afterwards.

4. Whilst we need to ensure accurate observation occurs, we also need to be as unobtrusive as possible. Prior to observation, establish whether you will be the 'fly on the wall' or whether you will engage in what Delamont and Hamilton (1982) call 'participant observation'. In infant classrooms, for example, it is likely that the observers will have to interact with eager young children.

5. For many teachers/colleagues, observation is a stressful and intrusive process and we need to handle the situation sensitively. The Department of Education and Science report (1989) has shown that despite the initial anxiety, teachers/colleagues have generally found observation to be a stimulating, rather than a daunting experience.

6. Absolute objectivity is impossible in any information-gathering procedure in the classroom. This limitation needs to be remembered.

7. One must accept a considerable loss of information when any reporting of classrooms takes place. Any observation system can only give a partial view of the classroom.

8. Beware of the inferences you make from observation data. If pupil A punches B on the nose this is factual data. One inference may be that pupil A is aggressive. If this is an isolated event, such an inference would be both inaccurate and damaging. If pupil B has provoked pupil A and we missed the incident the inference again would be inappropriate.

9. Beware of seeing what you want to see. If, for example, you don't like children who question what you say, an exceptionally able child in the class might be viewed as a nuisance or disruptive.

10. Wragg (1987) suggests that one potential problem is that of 'compensation' where the observer seeks to make up for his own deficiencies. Thus the observer who is untidy or badly organised may be excessively punitive over this characteristic in others.

11. Wragg (1987) also refers to the danger of 'projection' where the observer imagines himself actually teaching the class and thinks more in terms of what he would do in the circumstances rather than of the teacher being witnessed.

Other uses of the nudge sheet

1. The checklist has recently been used as part of a borough survey of primary schools to investigate the implementation of Key Stage 1 of the National Curriculum. On these occasions the maximum period of observation per classroom was 30 minutes. The nudge sheet has proved useful here in discussing with the teacher the elements of the curriculum that can be adapted for individual pupils.
    a. *Content*: whether a pupil's reading level, language abilities and prior experiences allowed her/him access to the task set.
    b. *Instructional strategies*: whether pupils were motivated to learn through the teaching approach offered.
    c. *Instrumental setting*: whether the group, class or individual approach used was the most appropriate for the pupil.
    d. *Student behaviour*: whether the behaviour exhibited (off task, lack of self-control etc.) needs to be addressed.
2. The checklist has been used in training advisers and advisory teachers in observation skills using video material. Any video showing a classroom in action is suitable. The series produced by the Inner London Education Authority (1983) is particularly applicable.
3. The checklist can be used by teachers over a period of time if necessary as a way of reviewing their own classroom practices, although they may need to share some aspects (for example, the physical setting) with colleagues.

Summary

In its report on school teacher appraisal nationally the DES (1989) stated that following classroom observation, immediate feedback and discussion had been shown to prompt teachers to reflect on their practice in the light of constructive comments of a highly focused kind.

The author would welcome correspondence from colleagues who are prepared to trial the nudge sheet and to identify ways in which it might be used and improved. I am particularly interested to hear from teachers who use it with their colleagues as a shared learning experience.

As a general rule the longer the time period available for observation, the more reliable the evidence gathered is likely to be. What is the optimum time for using the nudge sheet? Again how far can observers working in pairs overcome bias and inappropriate inferences and increase reliability of observation and recording? How far could the nudge sheet be adapted for observing in secondary schools?

I think I am superior to the common run of men in noticing things which escape attention, in observing them carefully.

(Charles Darwin)

References

Amidon, J. and Hough, J.B. (1967) *Interaction Analysis Theory Research and Application* New York: Addison-Wesley.

Croll, P. (1986) *Systematic Classroom Observation* Lewes: Falmer Press.

Croll, P. and Moses, D. (1985) *One in Five: The assessment and incidence of special education needs* London: Routledge and Kegan Paul.

Delamont, S. and Hamilton, D. (1982) 'Classroom research: A critique and new approach' in McCormick, R. (ed.) *Calling Education to Account* London: Heinemann Educational Books in association with the Open University Press.

Department of Education and Science (1989) *School Teacher Appraisal: A national framework* London: HMSO.

Flanders, N.A. (1970) *Analysing Teaching Behaviour* New York: Addison-Wesley.

Galton, M., Simon, B., and Croll, P. (1980) *Inside the Primary Classroom* London: Routledge and Kegan Paul.

Hopkins, D. and Bollington, R. (1989) *Evaluation and Research in Education*, **3**, (2).

Inner London Education Authority (1983) *Special educational needs: Observation of individual children* Videotapes.

Kounin, J.S. (1970) *Discipline and Group Management in the Classroom* New York: Holt, Rinehart and Winston.

Love, A.M. and Roderick, J.A. (1971) Teacher non-verbal communication: The development and field-testing of an awareness unit *Theory into Practice*, **10** (4).

Merrett, F. and Wheldall, K. (1986) *Observing Pupils and Teachers in Classrooms (OPTIC): A behavioural observation schedule for use in schools* Positive Products.

Mortimore, P., Sammons, P., Stoll, L., Lewis, D., and Ecob R. (1986) *The Junior School Project* London: ILEA Research and Statistics Branch.

Wragg, E. (1987) *Teacher Appraisal: A practical guide* Basingstoke: Macmillan Education.

Wragg, E. *et al.* (1983) *Systematic Classroom Interaction* Milton Keynes: Open University Press.

Future challenges

Mike Hinson

In the spring of 1991, London Weekend Television transmitted a series of six programmes entitled *Breadline Britain 1990s* which examined poverty in Britain through a number of case studies. As part of the series, MORI was commissioned to investigate people's views on what currently constitutes an unacceptably low living standard. Results of the survey reveal a wide measure of agreement on what those minimum standards should be. A full account, published in September 1991 by Harper Collins, shows that 11 million people (one in five of the population) are poor. This total includes more than three million children. Upwards of six million people are currently suffering a level of deprivation that affects their whole way of life.

The correlation between social deprivation and children with special educational needs has been recognised for many years. Regrettably, therefore, the ideal expressed in Gerry Lewis's chapter, that special needs teachers aim to work themselves out of a job by resolving children's learning difficulties, is still far from being achieved. From the foregoing chapters, readers will have concluded that substantial progress *has* been made in improving the quality of education for SEN pupils. Legislation is in place which recognises their equality of entitlement in curricular terms, also for the statementing of those with particular needs. Staff attitudes at all levels and across phases in education are gradually becoming more positive.

Notwithstanding, LMS has brought with it both worries and compensations. Its objective is to integrate resources and educational considerations into effective management practices. With the gradual introduction of delegated budgets, school resources are being costed on a common scale of finance. Yet resources remain finite and, as part of its annual planning cycle, each school must choose how to divide its total budget among the various expenditure headings, the most costly of which is 'staffing'. Observations show that, in this way, many headteachers are now prepared to allocate additional finance to special needs. There is always the worry that, in other schools, the reverse might happen. For example, with open enrolment, there could be the temptation to crowd out pupils with special needs in an attempt to obtain a 'higher quality' intake.

During 1990, Touche Ross Management Consultants undertook a feasibility study on behalf of the DES concerning the extension of local management to special schools (LMSS). Recognising that the education of pupils with learning difficulties is more costly than for other children, LEAs were recommended by the consultants to review their overall special needs provision. The consultants regarded LMSS as a way of obtaining a significant improvement in value for money, rather than as a way of making savings.

It seems, therefore, that local management of schools and the 'market place' philosophy are here to stay and that schools are beginning to adjust to the situation. Institutions can no longer concentrate their efforts solely on the well-being and development of pupils. They must also be cognizant of the fact that consumer demands and commercial development will, in future, have a greater influence in determining the nature of the service which they offer. It seems highly likely that the current drive for value for money will survive well into the next decade. whichever government is in power.

If any organisation is to make progress, it becomes necessary to undertake an evaluation of the tasks which it performs. In setting performance indicators, it is necessary to take into account the degree to which the school enables its pupils to overcome any form of social or educational disadvantage which they might have on entry, in other words the 'value added' to the pupil by the process of schooling. In her article 'Making indicators user-friendly', published in *Education*, 11 May 1990, researcher Kathryn Riley proposes a number of principles for what she prefers to term *school indicators* (measures for assessing the effectiveness and healthiness of schools):

— School indicators must be meaningful and easily com-
   municable to all partners in education.
— Clear and meaningful objectives and processes of assessment
   need to be developed in such a way that they are known to,
   and easily understood by the partners.
— Indicators should be comparable between schools in an LEA
   and a systematic data base developed.

— School indicators should be linked to the ethos and objectives of schools.
— Schools indicators should include both cognitive (academic) and non-cognitive (social) outcomes, such as pupils' self-concept in terms of self-esteem or confidence.
— School indicators should easily be implemented.
— They should be based on a systematic analysis of the consumer response to the quality and nature of the educational experience offered to all pupils, including those with special educational needs.

In order to complement school indicators, there is a need to establish other performance indicators which can be used to evaluate a person's professional progress. Schoolteacher appraisal has been on the agenda for some years now and came into effect in September, 1991. Teachers' general reactions to appraisal tend to be wary, since many view it rather as an adjudication of professional competence. The report of the National Steering Group, *School Teacher Appraisal: a National Framework* (DES 1989) underlines an earlier statement by ACAS that appraisal is a continuous and systematic process intended to help individuals with their professional development and career planning. Pilot objectives have revealed a number of benefits which accrue to both teachers and schools as a result of appraisal. These include: an improvement in teacher's morale and confidence; better professional relations and communications within schools; improved planning and delivery of the curriculum; wider participation in INSET, and better planning of professional development and career planning. It is envisaged that, with the introduction of appraisal for all teachers, these benefits would become available to them through 'a clear and open system operated with professionalism and sensitivity'. This being so, special needs teachers, with others, have little to fear, and possibly much to gain. In his chapter, John Visser has alerted us to the current situation concerning advanced training in special education. Government schemes for funding INSET have, so far, tended to be transient. It is likely that GEST will be replaced with a new set of regulations before we have accustomed ourselves to the present ones. The aims of appraisal could, therefore, be the means whereby special needs staff obtain appropriate funding to gain advanced specialist training.

As the profession becomes further embroiled with the educational market economy, schools will need to market themselves more than ever before. As defined by the Institute of Marketing, marketing is the management process for identifying, anticipating and satisfying customer requirements profitably. In the area of special educational needs, as in others, it will be necessary to identify the actual customers — are they the school staff, the governors, the parents or the LEA? Each has an obligation to the children; each has an influence on whether or not to 'purchase' the 'services' on offer. From a professional standpoint, children are the people to whom teachers are most emotionally committed. In order to fulfil their learning needs, SEN staff will have to stay in business. An element of pragmatism will be beneficial in achieving this end — they can best help the children by learning the skills of marketing. In some respects, those special needs staff who have actively engendered a whole-school approach have already taken the first steps in this direction. Having quitted the legendary broom cupboard, they are now marketing their considerable skills to a wider range of customers. Public relations is another aspect of marketing in which they have the foundation skills to succeed. Making the most of links within the community, both parents and governors, has already been discussed in this book.

The enduring commitment, expertise and enthusiasm of professionals who are concerned with children's special educational needs are still evident. Sweeping aside present frustrations, there remains a legislative foundation on which to build. By turning current trends in educational management to their own advantage, special educationalists have the key to positive progress in the future.

Index